eens
@ the library
series

# More Booktalking

## that works

Jennifer
Bromann

## Neal-Schuman Publishers, Inc.

New York                    London

*b 28418049*

Published by Neal-Schuman Publishers, Inc.
100 William Street, Suite 2004
New York, NY 10038

Copyright © 2005 Neal-Schuman Publishers

Printed and bound in the United States of America.

The paper used in this publication meets the minimum requirements of American National Standard for Information Sciences – Permanence of Paper for Printed Library Materials, ANSI Z39.48–1992.♾

**Library of Congress Cataloging-in-Publication Data**

Bromann, Jennifer.
    More booktalking that works / Jennifer Bromann.
        p. cm. — (teens@the library series)
    Includes index.
    ISBN 1-55570-525-1 (alk. paper)
    1. Young adults' libraries—Activity programs. 2. Book talks. 3. Libraries and teenagers. 4. Teenagers—Books and reading. 5. Reading promotion. I. Title. II. Teens @ the library series

Z718.5.B76 2005
027.62'6—dc22
                                                                2005002326

# Contents

# Series Editor's Foreword

*More Booktalking That Works* can help librarians bring the right book to the right reader at the right time. To achieve this feat, all you need to do is go out there and "sell" the book to a prospective teen reader, a simple job when a book advertises itself—all you have to do is display it. Maybe they see an attractive cover, find the subject matter engaging, embrace the style, or get connected by media or public events. Perhaps a reader learns about it naturally through word of mouth, or is a devotee of the author.

Other times the "sell" is not so easy. You must read the book, find something interesting to say, and describe it intriguingly. Did you make the teen reader want to know more? Inspire the reader enough to check out the book and begin to read it? Add an infinite number of books, styles of talks, and types of teen readers, and the procedure can become quite complex and daunting.

After working only a few years in a public library, Jennifer Bromann mustered the courage to write the original *Booktalking That Works*. I loved her moxie. I found her sure approach and certainty of technique astounding and her fresh ideas exciting!

Following the great success of her first book, *More Booktalking That Works* finds Ms. Bromann with several additional years of broadened professional experience—including work as a school library media specialist. This volume reviews basic assumptions, points out valuable tips, and teaches techniques that work with today's teen readers. It provides real-world-tested examples of booktalks you can adapt to your specific needs.

Joining the other excellent books in the *teens @ the library* series, *More Booktalking That Works*

- addresses the needs of youth-serving librarians and teachers in both public libraries and schools;
- draws from the best, most current research;
- targets the needs of today's changing teen population;

- cites the most innovative models;
- provides practical, tested solutions to common problems; and
- calls on each of us to realize the highest ideals of our profession.

The challenge of bringing books and teens together continues. Read young adult books, study great professional resources like this book, try to meet the needs of your booktalking audience, and then enjoy the sparks of synergy. You'll know you've done the job right when they come back asking for more!

Joel Shoemaker
Series Editor: *teens@ the library*

# Preface

Do you sometimes find booktalking stressful? Have you ever struggled, become tongue-tied, or run low on creativity? Have you ever read someone else's talk for inspiration? (Maybe going as far as to draft cards as scripts or memorizing them word-for-word?) After it was over, did you succeed and make the material appealing? Was your presentation interesting and lively? Were you able to do it again the next week? Ever wonder if you could truly master this skill?

One basic rule reigns over the secret to great booktalks: *make it your own*! Remember—the best booktalks sound natural, coming from your own ideas and said in your own words. Then why offer a manual of someone else's talks? Possibly you are new or returning to the profession and need to know what one should or could sound like. More likely, you want to talk a novel and no great ideas spring to mind for what you might use to sell it. Nothing leaps to life as a "good hook" to interest your patrons. The examples in this volume are intended to give you that all-important first hook so you can add your own summary—in your own words.

*More Booktalking That Works* shows how to ignite that initial interest in your audience. You can't always rely on "starting with talking"—especially with today's high percentage of reluctant readers. You may need to learn some "tricks of the trade" so students feel involved, pay attention, and wait for what you say next. You need to find out how to make them quick so you can continue without giving your audience a chance to be distracted.

Most of my talks are fairly short. If you wanted to memorize one you could, but I'd much rather have you embrace the *idea* in my talk. Use it to springboard your own notions based on what you remember and enjoyed about each book. And let it blossom into your own unique presentation.

The hooks suggested in *More Booktalking That Works* can often be used with similar treatments of the same topic. For example, if you tell fortunes to introduce *Gallow's Hill* by Lois Duncan, you can repeat the trick with any piece about the paranormal. If you ask students to define

different cliques for a discussion of *Tribes* by Arthur Slade, the definitions might be recycled with any book that mentions cliques. Group-
defined online-chat lingo can be used for books about technology or instant messaging. Get the idea? Think of *More Booktalking That Works*
as 200 different ways to start—and create—your own booktalks rather
than my scripts to recite word for word.

Part I, "Booktalking Q & A," is designed as an informal but informa-
tive real-world workshop. I based my answers on my own "in-the-field"
experiences. Other presenters might answer differently or tackle situations another way. Again, the point is ultimately to come up with your
own responses. (I can confirm my answers were created to make life
easier.) Part I centers around four big questions: "How Do I Create a
Successful Booktalk?"; "What Should I Know about Presenting a
Booktalk?"; "What Kinds of Books Make Good Booktalks?"; and "What
are Book Hooks and Quick Talks?" Along the way, I offer a spirited discussion of over 40 particular questions (including "Do I have to read
the whole book?" or "Can I booktalk books I don't love?" etc.).

Part II, "More Booktalking That Works" offers an array of all sorts of
possible books and all kinds of ideas for talks. The fundamental ideas:
construct generally short and snappy talks, always start with a way to in-
teract with the teens, and then relate it to something they know and care
about. Relate the material so students don't realize they are being en-
couraged to read a book. You're just telling them something that relates
to them or someone or something they know. Pull out the ideas of the
highest interest. It may not be the plot and it is not always what librarians and teachers liked most about the book. Part II ends with two indi-
ces to help you easily find the booktalks: genre/theme and title.

*More Booktalking That Works* is equally directed at both major ven-
ues of YA librarianship, public and school libraries. I worked at a public
library trying to get into the schools during the writing of the first book,
*Booktalking That Works*; now, I work at a high school and am still trying to get into the classrooms. After teaching a class called "Children's
Literature in a Multicultural Society" for teachers working on their cer-
tification, I read more multicultural titles. I also found an even greater
understanding of the struggles and issues of the underrepresented cultures in all literature but, in this case, young adult literature. Thus, I have
included more multicultural titles in this volume.

Feel free to use my suggestions any way that suits your needs. You
could take the booktalks word for word. You might use only the hooks.
You may perhaps use only the suggestions in the questions-and-answers
section. Or, you certainly can avail yourself of the ideas as you learn to
hone and make booktalks your own!

## REFERENCES

Bromann, Jennifer. 2001. *Booktalking That Works*. New York: Neal-Schuman.

Duncan, Lois. 1997. *Gallow's Hill*. New York: Delacorte Press.

Slade, Arthur. 2002. *Tribes*. New York: Wendy Lamb Books

# Part I

# Booktalking Q & A

# Q: How Do I Create
# a Successful Booktalk?

I will address the questions I usually receive when presenting workshops on booktalking. The answers are what have worked best for me in both public and high school libraries. I offer options to help in different situations; you will want to adapt them to what works best for you.

## WHAT ARE BOOKTALKS?

The concept of booktalking is essentially a simple idea. One person talks about specific books in order to encourage a particular audience to read. A successful booktalk will excite its audience to read, encourage them to look for specific titles of books, and help them discover new books on different subjects.

## HOW DO I CREATE A BOOKTALK?

In my previous book, *Booktalking That Works*, I describe in detail ten steps for writing a booktalk. Briefly, they include choosing a book teenagers can relate to, writing notes on memorable or especially thoughtful scenes, noting questions the book made you think of, reading the book jacket, writing both an introduction and conclusion for your booktalk, and then combining all this information to present to an audience.

## HOW DO I BEGIN A BOOKTALK PRESENTATION?

The main difference between my booktalks and some others I have read is how they start. Most talkers rely on plot, but anyone can come up with a summary of a book. It is true that most books can stand alone on their summary because the plots are so interesting. Some books, however, need a little more than just a summary to get the attention of your audience. Teens who are readers will find the books no matter what, and no matter how you present your booktalks they will find some of interest. But to get the attention of nonreaders or reluctant readers you have to find the best "hook" to catch their attention. A hook is my suggestion for how to start a booktalk. I discuss hooks in detail in the last question.

## HOW LONG SHOULD I TALK?

The length of presentations is very flexible, and it will depend in large part on the teacher. They can last anywhere from ten minutes to a whole class period. Be ready to accommodate any situation. If you are not going to use up the whole class period, you will have material for the presentations later in the semester. If students need time to select a book, you can allow for it. You can also offer an entire class period for teachers who would prefer that you use the whole time.

## HOW LONG SHOULD I TALK ABOUT ONE BOOK?

Booktalks can be anywhere from 30 seconds to about five minutes. Any longer might be too much to maintain your audience's interest. However, be prepared: booktalks can become longer when kids ask questions or offer responses, or when they seem interested and you share more of the story. Keep your spoken time short. You should just have an intro or hook and follow with a brief plot. Then see where your audience takes you.

## DO I NEED TO TALK QUICKLY?

I am a speed booktalker. I jump from one book to the next and probably talk faster than I should. In workshops, I generally talk faster to get as much in as possible in 45 minutes to an hour. In schools it goes a little slower because I often stop to listen to responses. In general, booktalks should be short and quick. You want to offer as many books as possible so the students have a greater selection. This will not only allow more variety, but it will lessen the chance of students' becoming bored if they are not interested in one of the books you have chosen or if they have already read it. Speed doesn't matter as long as you get the books in and the students hear about them, read them, or check them out.

## DO I NEED TO READ ALL THE BOOKS?

No. Of course it is best to read all the books you talk about and share with the students to guarantee their appropriateness and interest. However, other librarians read these books and review them and you can trust their advice. If you have a new book and haven't had time to read it, just briefly mention the plot. That is all I usually do after the hook anyway, even when I have read the whole book. You selected the books to read or ordered them for your library based on one review or summary. In the same way, teens don't need you to go on with details from the book unless you are sharing a particular scene.

Most of my booktalks involve a clever introduction to get the students' attention and then a brief summary. With quick booktalks for books I have not read, I essentially eliminate the introduction. Since I have not read the book I cannot as easily find those hidden connections, questions, and scenes upon which to draw. However, I still know what part of the plot piqued my interest, which means teens will probably be interested as well. It doesn't matter if you read ALL the books as long as you can accurately and briefly describe the plot. If you didn't, start by saying that these are all books you have read; you are not lying. You are simply tacking a few books on to the end to offer more selections of books you may or may not have wanted to read. For example, this is how I once described the book *Dr. Franklin's Island*, which at that time I had not yet read: "These kids win a science contest and are traveling to another country to be part of a project. Their plane crashes and they think the guy living on the island where they land will help them, but instead he wants to use them in experiments to turn them into animals." It is simple, but it describes the exciting plot. There is absolutely nothing wrong with presenting some books you have not read.

## ANY SUGGESTIONS FOR HOW TO READ AS MANY BOOKS AS POSSIBLE?

When multiple teachers ask for different booktalks more than once a year, especially if they have some of the same students, it can be difficult for many librarians to keep up. If you have side projects, a full-time job, are going back to school, or have a family, there may be little time to read a variety of books. The high school where I work started a new mandatory reading program for freshmen. Students in this class are required to read one or more books with a partner. Because of this, I created a list of all the books that our library has more than one copy of. After handing out this list, I was asked to booktalk specific selections to a class with only a few days' notice. I had not read all of these books. I cannot read at work. I was teaching two night classes and taking a weekend class that semester while finishing this book. So I booktalked the ones I did know. I referred to the teacher who had read some of the other books. And for the remaining titles, I simply said, "Now I have not read this, but I heard it is about. . . . " Many booktalkers say that you should never talk about books you have not read. You can decide what you feel comfortable with, but keep in mind that others don't always read every word of every book they share, and it is okay if you do not either.

## SHOULD I USE PREWRITTEN, OR PREPUBLISHED, BOOKTALKS?

You shouldn't. I couldn't. I have a poor memory and it would take me a day to memorize a booktalk someone else had written. The point of the booktalk is just to get an idea and decide where to place your focus. Come up with an idea for a clever start, interesting questions to ask, or just follow an outline. If you have read the book you can create a summary on your own. The problem? Sometimes you don't have the time to devote to hours of creating opening or closing hooks or deciding what part of a book to focus on. *More Booktalking That Works* focuses on that idea by offering a suggestion on how to start a booktalk for each book. This is what I call a book hook. No memorization is necessary. Pick an opening, and then keep talking from there with as much information as you are comfortable with sharing. This technique will also help the booktalk be more conversational. A memorized booktalk, or one that is read, can sometimes sound like a lecture. Have you ever seen a preview for a movie and then didn't laugh when you saw it because the funny parts had already been revealed in the trailer? Why would anyone want to read a book if they already know all the good parts?

## SHOULD I INCLUDE A VARIETY OF GENRES AND CULTURES?

It is definitely best to include as many subjects and genres as you can, but you have to be practical. Think about your audience. If you were to be politically correct each time and include a book for every culture and topic, you might not be using your best books or giving your best booktalks, and you might not satisfy your audience. That goal is unrealistic because you could never finish.

When presenting to adults, I try to include several multicultural books in my presentations since I never know which members of which communities will be present. You know your school and community. Still, you never know who might be in your group. You might like to include a diverse selection because you never know if there might be a Native American or Latino student in your class. Just be careful to not throw in a book simply because it has a character from a particular ethnicity. Evaluate each book for sensitivity and stereotypes, and, then, pick the best. Remember, multicultural titles are not only for people of specific cultures, but to promote a better understanding of diversity and acceptance for all students and even some teachers.

After you've done a few booktalks and see which books the kids in your area want, then it will be easier for you to know how to divide your talk. Even if there isn't a big demand for science fiction in your groups, you can still add one each time to intrigue those who may develop an interest—or at least an interest in the book you have selected. Even though some teens will like specific genres, it is always best to include some nonfiction and basic teen life/angst books about everyday teenager life. This will increase your chances at gaining the interest of the majority of your audience. If you haven't been reading multicultural books or books on specific genres, remember that you can always quickly mention a few with the basic plot summaries at the end of your booktalks. Select books with universal themes that will appeal to many. In a high school, you will have to read a variety of YA and adult books. Come prepared with some classics, best sellers, and books by well-respected authors for your older readers. I personally have had to put my adult-book reading to the side to make time satisfy the needs of the freshman reading classes. You can read several young adult books in the time it would take you to read one of the most bestselling novels.

## SHOULD I USE A THEME?

It is best to not limit yourself to one theme. It seems artificial to force a book to fit a theme. If a teacher requests historical fiction, or another specific topic, that would be the time to show you are flexible. Offer several possible themes. Not limiting yourself to a theme allows you to select a greater variety and to use your best books or the books for which you have the most booktalks.

## SHOULD I EVER READ ALOUD FROM THE BOOKS?

Try to have more variety rather than reading from every book you present. I know many booktalkers read with success, but I'm not a big fan of that technique. I suggest you start off with a hook, then read, memorize, or recite a small passage. Continuously reading from book after book just might get tedious. I am only talking about booktalks when I talk about not reading too much. Reading aloud to a classroom is certainly an excellent way to introduce students to literature, the way a book should be read, as well as the vocabulary and sentence structure. When using booktalks, however, find those shorter gripping passages and simply add to them. Always be aware that reading aloud from each book you present may not be engaging enough for most teen readers.

## SHOULD I MENTION THE AUTHOR'S NAME?

No. I have several reasons for not always giving the author's name in my booktalks. The first is that my memory doesn't always allow me to recall it at the right moment without checking out the book cover. The second is that kids don't care. They usually won't remember. And the third is that giving the author's name reminds students you are talking about a book per se. A good booktalk should just pique a student's interest in finding out more.

## SHOULD I GIVE AWAY THE ENDING?

You should rarely give away the ending of the book unless it is something known or unless there is still some twist left to the end that you are not revealing. Don't be tempted to always tell the best parts of the stories. Tell enough to get the students interested and then leave them to discover the secrets on their own.

## SHOULD I EVER USE PROPS?

I rarely use props in high school because it takes too much time and it seems a bit childish to me. You can certainly use props to help connect an idea or a plot to a student, but they are usually more effective with younger readers. Sometimes I can't resist. They are most effective if you can find a way to relate the prop naturally to the book and the students. For example, I have used an ink pad to take fingerprints of students for a book on forensic science and Scrabble™ letters for the book *Word Freak* by Stefan Fastis.

## HOW DO I DETERMINE THE RIGHT AGE LEVEL?

In *Booktalking That Works* and *More Booktalking That Works*, grade levels are indicated with each booktalk. You may decide differently, depending on the culture of your school. If absolutely no mention of sex is considered appropriate in your school, you may have to reconsider some of the books with a middle-school rating. YA books with no sexual content or no profanity might be appropriate for fifth or sixth grade, and you might find that there are middle-school books that appeal to older students.

My experience is that most books marketed for young adults are appropriate for high school students and seventh and eighth graders. I usually reserve adult books for high school unless there is no sex or adult content at all and the book could be easily understood by a general audience.

It is easier to defend a decision to purchase a young adult book based only on the reviews than to buy an adult book for a young adult collection without reading it first. A young adult book is written and marketed specifically for one age group, and the reviews will usually tell you if there is anything that is inappropriate for certain readers. Reviews of adult books, on the other hand, are not likely to mention if there is anything inappropriate for younger readers, for example, sex, because that is not an issue for adult readers. So read adult books yourself if you want to booktalk them to young adults. I also look at the grade levels that book reviewers gave the books. This sometimes helps expand or narrow the age range I use them for. Your ratings may be different from mine. You also have to consider that you may be talking to lower-level classes, and they need a variety for their various reading abilities.

## DO I HAVE TO REMEMBER CHARACTER NAMES?

People are surprised that I don't always use characters' names when I booktalk. I am more likely to say "this guy" or "a teenager" rather than "Carrie" or "Steve." I confess: This is because I have a poor memory and don't always remember names. I sometimes forget a name as soon as I put down the book. A woman at a workshop told me that she was glad I did that because she has trouble remembering names, too. Remember, there are no real rules in booktalking. I have some I go by, and other booktalkers have those they go by, but you really have to do what works for you. Teenagers will not notice that you don't give names, or, if they ask, say you forgot and look at the book jacket.

# Q: What Should I Know about Presenting a Booktalk?

## I AM A SOLO LIBRARIAN. HOW DO I FIND TIME TO BOOKTALK?

If you are the only librarian running a media center, and you have no support staff, you might ask a class to come to the library so you can still supervise. In this case, you might want to only booktalk for 10 or 15 minutes so you can get back to the other students needing your services in the library. Perhaps you could ask the teacher to run circulation or assist students while you booktalk. Consider closing the library for one day a semester to visit the different classes requesting your services.

## I AM A SCHOOL LIBRARIAN. HOW DO I GET INTO CLASSROOMS?

This is one of the most commonly asked questions, and it was also addressed in *Booktalking That Works*. It is a challenge, but it is easier for a school librarian because you know the teachers and they know you. Also, you can come on short notice. Send memos or e-mails to the English teachers and offer your services. Many who have silent reading time will especially appreciate your offer. Write it up in your library or school newsletter or wherever teachers might read it. This is where you will get other teachers interested. If you have booktalks on a specific topic, such as historical fiction or self-help books, send the memo to teachers in those fields. Listen to conversations and pay attention to the curriculum; offer future services to other teachers. Ask them if they would be interested in booktalks on a specific topic and tell them when you might have books prepared to talk about. When teachers register for library space for sustained silent reading (SSR) or time for their students to select books, be sure to offer your services. Explain exactly what it is you do, since many teachers will not have heard the word "booktalk" before.

Then, just by word of mouth, you will soon be getting others interested in having you visit their classes. Teachers at my school now ask to reserve time before school even starts.

## I AM A PUBLIC LIBRARIAN. HOW DO I GET INTO SCHOOLS?

As a public librarian it is more difficult. In fact, some librarians find it so challenging that they are discouraged from trying. Teachers will not come to you unless they have heard you before or unless the previous librarian has spoken to their classes before. It is easy to sit back and let the school librarian handle it, which might be what the teachers and school library media specialists want, but you should always make the effort. Invite school librarians to the public library for a meeting so that you can offer your services and find out what they do in their schools. If this does not work for you, arrange individual meetings with the librarians at their schools. If they are excited about your offer, see if they can arrange the class visits for you or arrange for you to visit the library when the students are there. This is a benefit of schools that do not have flexible scheduling. The school librarian will know when each age group will be in the library and will often welcome an outside visitor for the day.

If school librarians do not seem receptive, and if they love doing their own booktalks, as they should, let them. Even though it is good for students to hear different approaches to booktalking and hear about books that might not be available in the school library, it is the school librarian's territory, and the teachers may not want you to take up too much of their hectic schedules. They may only want students to read books that are in the school library. This is their decision. But don't give up yet; see if you can work with the school librarians. Ask if you could do some tandem booktalking or alternate between talking about books in the public library and books in the school library. If there is still no welcome and you know the librarian already does his or her own booktalks, it would be unwise to do an end run and immediately start asking teachers and the principal.

Otherwise, wait until next year, and see if there is a new librarian. Find out the exact names of English teachers and call them or send them letters. One way that can sometimes work well is to call the principals, especially if you have worked with them before doing other types of visits. Sometimes they can arrange for you to pop into the classrooms. If nothing else, and you really want to use your booktalking skills, try slipping a few booktalks in when you visit to promote the summer reading or volunteer program. Try private schools that may or may not have a full-time librarian. Try adding booktalks to the beginning or end of your programs. Offer to do booktalks in your own neighborhood on your time off. There are many ways you can still booktalk even if you can't get into a classroom. Still, if you absolutely cannot get into a school, don't be afraid to give up. It is okay if you can't visit every school.

## WHAT DO I DO IF STUDENTS WON'T STOP TALKING?

Teachers can often be helpful in getting the students back on task. Usually I do not worry if kids continue to talk. I believe that this means they are interested in what you are saying even if it is not directly related to a book—as long as they are talking about the book or something you said. Once you get started with a new book, question, or topic, they will most likely follow along. If you still find that asking questions does not work for you, change the questions to statements. So instead of "What would you do . . . ," say "These students did this. . . . "

## WHAT IF STUDENTS WON'T ANSWER MY QUESTIONS?

In a smaller setting, I almost always have at least one student who likes to joke around and answer the questions with which I begin many of my booktalks. However, larger groups are another story. I once spoke to three classes at once that were spread throughout the whole library. The students wanted to appear cool in front of the others, and it was such a large space that they often answered the questions at their own tables but would not share with the entire group. All you can do is answer the question yourself and move on. If this occurs several times, give up on the questions and simply give the plot or change your booktalking technique to a scenario. If you do this quickly without allowing much waiting time for responses, the students won't even notice if you are a bit frazzled. You can say something like, "Well, in this book . . . " and give the answer as it occurred in the book you are discussing without any of the students' responses.

## IS THERE A LIMIT TO THE NUMBER OF CLASSES I CAN PRESENT TO AT ONE TIME?

When considering how many classes to speak to at a time you need to do what is comfortable for you. Booktalking to one class is certainly preferable, but you also don't want to turn people away. If you are visiting a school, you may only be offered one hour during the day. In this case, speaking to multiple classes is the only way you can reach a significant number of students. If you are in a school, suggest another day. If this does not work for some teachers, do what you can to accommodate them so they will continue to return for more.

## HOW OFTEN SHOULD I VISIT A CLASSROOM OR A SCHOOL?

You can visit a classroom or a school as often as you are invited to do so and as long as you have enough books to share. If teachers request your services more often than you have time to read new books, you might want to try the suggestions for quick talks that I give later on and cut your booktalks to 10 or 15 minutes.

## WHAT DO I DO SO STUDENTS REMEMBER THE BOOKTALK?

A bookmark is one of the best ways to remind students about the books you presented. It can easily be folded into a pocket, book, notebook, or wallet. Keep extras at the circulation, youth services, adult services, or young adult services desks—or all of these—depending on where your students go to seek information. Many teenagers will return to ask for the books with or without the bookmark and with or without an exact title. It also helps the presenter remember which books were talked about each time and to which set of students. Keep the bookmarks on file, and write the teacher's or school's name on the back along with dates and class periods or whatever will help. The whole library staff will appreciate this reminder in your absence. For older teens, remember that bigger is not better. They may be too embarrassed to return to the library with a huge brochure of annotated books you have prepared for them. A simple bookmark or one-page list would be the best reminder. And . . . it is also more difficult to turn a bookmark into a proper paper airplane.

One problem with creating a bookmark or handout is that you might not be sure which books you will be using. You may have several classes in a day or a week, and many of your books may disappear off your cart or shelves very quickly. You could, instead, prepare an extensive booklist of all the books you usually talk about and have the students mark the ones that interest them. You could also use this to keep track of the books you talked about by checking them off your list as you go or after your presentation.

## HOW SHOULD I HANDLE MULTIPLE REQUESTS FOR A BOOK FOLLOWING A BOOKTALK?

There is no good answer for this question. You already know that, if possible, you can order multiple copies, you can have waiting lists, or you can talk about multiple books to different classes. One solution was to buy my own copies of the books to free up copies in the library while I am talking. If I needed to give my personal copy away, I would, and I would replace it later if it was destroyed. However, I give workshops on this topic, so I use them again and again.

Others have made PowerPoint® slide shows or overheads of the books they talk about and use those rather than the actual books to make more copies of the books available to the students. You might also consider interlibrary loaning copies of books you will be using if it is possible to do so from your library system and if there is enough time for students to return the books without penalty. I often borrow books from the other high school in our district when I know I will be booktalking.

After a few years of booktalking some of the same books, you will know which are popular with your audience and you can simply buy multiple copies of those books. You will soon be able to tell from reading reviews the types of books that will be popular and you can purchase multiple copies ahead of time. On your bookmark or handout you might also put the title of a similar book or another book by that author under each title, in case the book is in high demand. If you don't have time to read multiple books and prepare multiple booktalks, or your budget doesn't allow for multiple books, just don't worry. If you have provided a list or bookmark to kids, those who really want the books will eventually find them. After I left my last position, one of the librarians called me because a student was asking for a book I used for a scary stories session two years earlier. Be available after you talk to share other ideas for those who did not find a book during your presentation. The students walking out of your booktalking session with no books will have to rely on your further suggestions, the displays you have, and the other books available in the library. That is why you share a lot of books, buy a lot of books, and know about a lot of books.

## SHOULD I WORRY IF KIDS DON'T FINISH A BOOK?

I was concerned at first when I saw a class visit the library for sustained silent reading and put the books back on the shelves after they read for 20 minutes. They may be reading each week, but they never finish anything. This practice is no longer considered to be as important as it once seemed. After all, adults often read only half of a magazine article, and they put books down all the time. We stop watching movies halfway through or start them in the middle. One hopes that a good booktalk introduces books the students will want to read all the way through. Booktalks also give you the chance to share books that they don't have to read all the way through, for example a book of poetry or short stories, or a nonfiction book with many sections, such as *Hidden Secrets* or *Live from New York*. It is great if they finish a book, but you have to lead the way by providing a variety of books.

## WHY DON'T SOME TEENS READ?

Teenagers are the hardest audience to reach. They are the ones who would rather sleep, talk, or stare into space in the library rather than pick up a book. This is okay. We know that many do read. We know that many teenagers later become readers. And we know that many still become successful by reading what they need to know for their professions or for general information, but not necessarily fiction. Some don't have time. Some have other interests. Some just don't have the attention span.

## HOW DO I REACH THE RELUCTANT READER?

It is best to offer some books where they can just read parts, not the whole thing. With *Live from New York*, I tell students to just pick out the sections about cast members they like. With something like *Don't Sweat the Small Stuff for Teens*, I tell them to pick the areas they would like to learn more about. Reading doesn't necessarily have to mean completing a whole book. Many classroom teachers are using newspaper and magazine articles to get kids reading and to enhance their knowledge about subjects related to the class content. A perfect booktalking session will involve adult books, teen books, short books, and nonfiction, with various genres and cultures represented. My booktalking sessions are never perfect. Often I am limited to the books that are available for that class at that time and what I have been reading lately. But it is best to have something for all abilities so students don't tune you out when they see the length of the books and to have something for all interests so students don't think you are only speaking to one group of students.

## HOW DO I DETERMINE THE READING INTEREST?

From being in a variety of schools doing student teaching or observations, and by being around other librarians and asking questions, it is apparent that every school has a different reading culture. Naturally, each student will have different reading tastes, but it is surprising that different schools have different overall preferences. At that school where I student taught, the students were more into bestsellers and adult books. They often requested Oprah books. My current position is in a school where over the years little focus was placed on fiction. My first goal was to update the fiction collection. I first selected all my favorites and the books I had booktalks for. Then I consulted best-book lists from ALA. I purchased Oprah books, not because of their popularity, but because many of the titles and authors she had chosen were books or authors on my college reading lists. They are authors whose names will be around for many years. Next I chose books by popular authors whose names often appear on the bestsellers list. I could not believe that only a couple Stephen King books were on the shelves, for example. Students who in the past sought out Harry Potter or Nicholas Sparks had been previously disappointed until I updated the shelves. The database Novelist was used to compile lists of popular authors' titles, although simple Web searches or large library online catalogs could yield the same results. The last step was to keep up with current bestsellers and the most talked about and best reviewed YA books.

In my current high school position, I was not sure at first what students wanted to read. Now I have a better idea. It seems that the most popular books are YA books. This surprised me because I thought these were the books they got in junior high and they might now be ready for something more advanced. Your situation may be unusual. Because of what I have seen and heard about other high schools, I now believe there must be a variety of books. You cannot label high school students as only wanting to read a certain level or genre of book. In my situation, adult choices were hardly touched unless they were by popular bestselling authors, otherwise the students wanted short books about teens. One student would read a short YA book and hand it in by the end of the day and check out two more. Most students want fast and quick. Many look for the shortest books they can find. There are, of course, those who do want books like Lord of the Rings or *The Hitchhiker's Guide to the Galaxy*. I have a lunchtime book club for my high school students. I try to select short books because they have trouble finishing the books. I also alternate between longer and shorter books or books they might have already read. For *Harry Potter* I said they could come even if they just saw the movie. We also read *Maus*, which as a graphic novel seemed less daunting to read. Be flexible.

## HOW DO I DECIDE WHAT MIX OF GENRES TO KEEP IN MY COLLECTION?

There are those who want science fiction/fantasy series, and there are those who only want manga. A little of every genre is necessary. Bottom line: In my school library, the focus of my collection has been young adult books since that is what goes off the shelf most frequently. The public library where I previously worked did not have a separate YA section. The books were shelved with the adult fiction. You know your students and collection, but it is important to remember that every student, school, and town may be different. Try to find out about your patrons. In a survey (see Figure 1) I asked eight hundred high school students at Lincoln-Way Central High School in New Lenox, IL, about their reading interests. I sent it to teachers to distribute to their classes to get an idea of what teens read: The results that follow in Figure 2 show my particular findings. My high school students seem to prefer YA books. However interesting the results, do not use these numbers when building your collection to decide what percentage of books you need in each subject or genre. If 50% want mysteries, what if the 12% who want fantasy are 90% of your readers? Surveys just give a rough idea of where the interests lie, but the library and librarian must provide something for everyone. This survey was given before our collection was updated. Circulation has since increased.

Figure 1. Survey Questions

# What Do You Like to Read? Survey

Have you read a book for fun that was not assigned by a teacher this school year?  Y  N

Have you ever checked out a book to read for fun from your school library?  Y  N

From your public library?  Y  N

Please place a check next to **ALL** the types of books you like to read.

\_\_\_ Sports fiction
\_\_\_ True sports stories
\_\_\_ Graphic novels/Comic books
\_\_\_ Classics
\_\_\_ Mystery
\_\_\_ Science fiction
\_\_\_ Fantasy
\_\_\_ Poetry
\_\_\_ True crime
\_\_\_ Horror/Scary
\_\_\_ Romance
\_\_\_ Humor/Funny
\_\_\_ Adventure
\_\_\_ History
\_\_\_ Historical fiction
\_\_\_ Biographies
\_\_\_ Music/TV/Movies
\_\_\_ Science
\_\_\_ Short stories
\_\_\_ Teen problems/Life
\_\_\_ Realistic fiction
\_\_\_ Religion
\_\_\_ Plays
\_\_\_ Diaries/Journals
\_\_\_ Books with teen characters
\_\_\_ Books with adult characters
\_\_\_ Other _____

What is your favorite book?  _____

Thanks
The Lincoln-Way Central Library

## Figure 2. Survey Results

| Lincoln-Way Central High School Reading Interest Survey |
|---|
| 828 English students surveyed (Fall 2002) |

| Have you read a book for fun that was not assigned by a teacher this school year? | | |
|---|---|---|
| | Number of Students | Percentage |
| Yes | 454 | 55% |
| No | 374 | 45% |

| Have you ever checked out a book to read for fun from your school library? | | |
|---|---|---|
| Yes | 157 | 19% |
| No | 667 | 81% |

| From your public library? | | |
|---|---|---|
| Yes | 476 | 57% |
| No | 352 | 43% |

| Favorite genres/Subjects | | |
|---|---|---|
| Humor/Funny | 439 | 53% |
| Mysteries | 387 | 47% |
| Horror/Scary | 368 | 45% |
| Adventure | 344 | 42% |
| Music/TV/Movies | 334 | 41% |
| Teen problems/Life | 325 | 39% |
| Fantasy | 306 | 37% |
| True crime | 272 | 33% |

Figure 2. (continued)

| | | |
|---|---|---|
| Romance | 250 | 30% |
| History | 209 | 25% |
| Realistic fiction | 208 | 25% |
| Poetry | 205 | 25% |
| Science fiction | 203 | 25% |
| Diaries/Journals | 197 | 24% |
| Classics | 186 | 23% |
| Graphic novels/Comic books | 179 | 23% |
| True sports stories | 185 | 22% |
| Biographies | 174 | 21% |
| Sports fiction | 159 | 19% |
| Short stories | 156 | 19% |
| Historical fiction | 136 | 17% |
| Religion | 77 | 9% |
| Plays | 73 | 9% |
| Science | 31 | 7% |
| Books with teen characters | 307 | 37% |
| Books with adult characters | 184 | 22% |

# Q: What Kinds of Books Make Good Booktalks?

While all books could be booktalked, some types are better than others. Here are my top 20 types of books that make the best booktalks.

1. Funny books. Use a funny part from the story, like how the boy would never get tackled in *Son of the Mob* because they thought the mob family would go after the players.
2. Short stories. You can focus on only one story and say, "This is just one of the stories in . . ." You don't want to give away the plot of all the stories after all.
3. Nonfiction books. Besides the fact that boys have been known to prefer nonfiction, use more novelty nonfiction with short sections, such as books about musical groups or weird occurrences. You only have to share a few.
4. Scary books. Turn a scene into a ghost story.
5. Books in verse. The students can read these quickly—and so can you. Therefore, they are easy for you to promote. Stress that they don't sound like poetry.
6. Books in a series. You only have to read one book in the series, but you can use that as your talk for all the books in a series.
7. Sports books. It is usually easy to find an example for a talk based on a real sports figure or team.
8. Short books. If nothing else, the length will interest students. You can simply say you finished it in under an hour.
9. Biographies. It is easy to pull out a few interesting facts about a person's life for a simple booktalk. One warning: your booktalk may already be out of date the next year.
10. Children's books. Some children's books will work with teens, such as *Through My Eyes* by Ruby Bridges, *Bone Detectives* by Donna Jackson and Charlie Fellenbaum, and even *Bed Bed Bed* by the musical group They Might Be Giants. These books may not count

for a book report, but they could be a quick read for sustained silent reading (SSR).

11. Books with a twist. Leave your audience hanging before you reveal the shocking ending.

12. Books with mature topics. You don't even have to tell students what *God of Beer* by Garret Keizer is about. They will pick up books with titles like this—or like *The True Meaning of Cleavage* by Mariah Fredericks and *On the Bright Side, I Am Now the Girlfriend of a Sex God* by Louise Rennison—just by the title alone. Boys will sometimes even pick up the latter out of curiosity. Books on sexuality also intrigue students.

13. Books based on a movie. You might avoid reading or sharing these because students have already seen the movie. However, even just a mention may help students by offering them something familiar. Most will attempt to read the book and not cheat if it is as interesting to them as the movie was. *Friday Night Lights* flew off the shelves after the movie was released. It had many teen fans.

14. Books written in unique formats. This new trend is popular with students. They seem to like the idea of reading a book in e-mails, letters, or instant messages.

15. Lists. It is easy to pull out sections from books that contain lists, surveys, or questions to use for a booktalk.

16. Read-a-likes. Students love books like *Go Ask Alice,* published anonymously, or *Speak* by Laurie Halse Anderson. Be prepared with some books that are similar to the popular books in your school.

17. Books you have read. Even though they might not have wide appeal, share some books you have read for personal enjoyment or knowledge that are not marketed for your audience, such as books on gardening or politics. This allows you to have more booktalks and use your personal reading time to help you at work.

18. The supernatural. Many students love books with ESP and ghosts. It is easy to start these books with fortune-telling, mind reading, or stories of real ghosts and soothsayers.

19. Books with choices. This doesn't necessarily have to be a book where the reader makes choices, although it can be. It could also be a book where the characters make choices. Your booktalks can suggest these choices or solutions and leave the reader wondering what decisions the characters will make.

20. Books written by teenagers. Promote a book by telling your audience the book was written by someone their own age.

# Q: What are Book Hooks and Quick Talks?

## WHAT IS A BOOK HOOK?

Book hooks are ideas that pique interest and grab the attention of your audience. Simply describing a book is not usually enough. Anyone can come up with a summary of a book. And you'll find some teens won't listen to a booktalk or take it seriously no matter how great the book. Often you need to trick them. Dazzle them with book hooks.

## HOW DO I USE THEM?

The best type of hook is beginning with something that makes the teens think that you are talking about them or their friends or someone in the news or movies—anyone but a character in a book. Then when you get them interested you tie it into a book before they even realize what has happened. The following questions are about types of hooks that were originally presented in *Booktalking That Works*, but which are revisited here to give you a better idea of how to make this happen in your booktalks. (If I've piqued your interest, see my first book *Booktalking That Works* for a detailed ten-step plan for writing a booktalk.)

## HOW DO I HOOK USING MOOD?

The most important thing to remember about mood is that you don't want to pretend to be a professor of English literature. Don't talk about the dreariness or the damp or the smoky air. To present mood to teens you can either read aloud or memorize short quotes from the book that represent the mood or tone the author intended or speak in a style that represents the mood, such as speaking really fast to represent a teenager or very slowly to represent a scary story.

## HOW DO I HOOK USING CHARACTERS?

Once again, forget the professor. Don't describe how the characters look and their characteristics. Focus on how you want to represent the people in the story to the teens. Some booktalkers speak successfully in the first person, and this works best with a younger audience and for those presenters who are skilled in dramatics. For those who are not skilled actors, it is best to speak in the second or third person. If you speak in the second person, you put the focus on the teens. "You were at this party..." You put them in the place and situations of the characters, and for a moment they imagine themselves in the book. If this doesn't work for you, or if you do not want to do this for books with heavier issues such, as single parenthood or suicide, you can use the third person. By saying, "There was this guy..." you get teens to begin to think of the character as a real person, someone they might know in a middle school or high school similar to their own.

## HOW DO I HOOK USING PLOT?

Plot can usually carry the book on its own. You can just add a simple plot summary to the end of your booktalk or begin this way. Sometimes you will have already told the plot by the other ways you started the booktalk, in which case there is no need for any more.

## HOW DO I HOOK USING SCENES?

Once again, avoid detailed descriptions. Teenagers do not need to hear about how the old castle looked unless there is something very unusual about the environment. In this case scene refers more to pulling out a scene from the book. It is about focusing on a chapter or one event in the life of any of the characters in a book. It does not need to be the most significant, but it does need to be one of the most entertaining or interesting.

## HOW DO I HOOK USING QUESTIONS?

You can always think of a question. What you don't want to do is ask a question about the book. The kids haven't read it yet. They can't tell you what Robert should do if they have not yet experienced his actions and character. They can, however, comment on what they would do in certain situations. So if you say, "What would you do if...," they are answering for themselves, and then you can tie their answers into how similar or different they are from what happens in the book. If you create your own scenario to start a booktalk, you can ask what most teens would do in that situation. If you speak in the second person and put the teens in the place of the characters, you can ask them what *they* would do. If you can't think of another hook, a question will almost always work.

## HOW DO I HOOK USING CONNECTIONS?

The best way to present booktalks is to somehow relate books to the students themselves. This can be done through pop culture, world events, or their own lives. Ask if they have seen a movie or TV show that relates to the book in some way. Talk about a current reality show or movie that even slightly relates to a book. Mention famous people. Watch the news or news-magazine shows to find stories teens might have heard of that relate to the books. For example, there was a story about a Chicago radio station, 103.5 KISS-FM. It seems that a bank robber called the station to confess a crime. The FBI took clues from the call and was able to catch the thief. In the book *I Am the Messenger* by Markus Zusak (2005), a boy starts getting playing cards in the mail with messages about things he is to do. This begins after he stopped a bank robbery from occurring. You can also use something like a school dance that teens are involved in at the time or a situation everyone goes through, like not having homework done, asking someone on a date, feeling left out at a party or event, or getting ready for the prom, even if you make up the situation. Look for contemporary stories in the news that may relate to books from the past. An older book is still new to a student who has not read it before, especially if you can relate it to current events.

## WHAT ARE QUICK TALKS?

Quick talks are really short booktalks or brief plot summaries. They simply state the basic plot of a book with no details or hooks. The quick talks in this section will give you an idea about what you can say for books you have not read, books you don't remember, books that confused you, books you could only make it part way through, new books you had no time to read, or books you had no interest in reading but that teens might like.

## HOW SHORT ARE QUICK TALKS?

If you are in a time crunch or you need more books, you can always quickly mention some that you have not read. I often say that sometimes you will just not be able to find a hook for a particular talk no matter how hard you work on it. And sometimes you may want to talk about a book you read long ago, even before you were in college or before you started to write and present booktalks. In these cases, all you have to do is simply say one to three sentences about a book. These sentences should briefly sum up the main idea of the book; they should tell a book's unique plot without giving away any surprises.

## WHY SHOULD I USE QUICK TALKS?

Sometimes less is more. Even though these talks are short, they are often just enough to interest some students. Students often check out the books about which I only say one sentence. Often that is all you need. Sometimes I even do it for books I have read and loved and remember details about. I might not have time to go into detail, or I realize that my audience will not appreciate the booktalk I have prepared. If you don't have enough time, just chop the first half of your booktalk off and tell the class the plot. That might be just the punch needed to leave kids guessing. You might have two classes at the same time and each student has to take a book you talk about, so you need to squeeze a lot of books into your time frame. Don't be afraid to use a short summary when you have to present more books, you have a new book you haven't had time to read and you know kids will love, you just can't think of a hook or a good intro, or you just can't quite remember the details about a book you read and liked. You want a variety anyway. Mix short talks in between longer ones.

## WHAT ARE SOME EXAMPLES OF QUICK TALKS?

These are ten books I have either never read or have not read in a long time. The examples show how you might present a quick booktalk from just reading the book jacket and book reviews or from skimming the books.

Etchemendy, Nancy. 2000. *The Power of Un*. Chicago: Front Street.
A boy gets a machine called The Unner, which helps him erase the mistakes he has made in his life.

Giberga, Jane Sughrue. 1997. *Friends to Die For*. New York: Puffin Books.
In this story a party gets crazy and one of the friends is murdered; they then have to find out who the murderer is.

Haddix, Margaret Peterson. 2003. *Escape from Memory*. New York: Simon & Schuster.
In *Escape from Memory*, a girl agrees to be hypnotized by her friends at a slumber party, only she starts remembering scary things from her past.

Halam, Ann. 2003. *Dr. Franklin's Island*. New York: Laurel Leaf.
Some kids win a science contest and are traveling to another country to be part of a project. Their plane crashes and they think the guy living on the island where they land will help them, but instead he wants to use them in experiments to turn people into animals.

Jenkins, A. M. 2003. *Out of Order*. New York: HarperCollins.
A boy will no longer be able to play baseball unless he can raise his GPA to a C. To do this he has to be tutored by the new girl in school who has green hair and who seems much more interesting than his girlfriend.

Lynch, Chris. 2001. *Freewill*. New York: HarperCollins.
In *Freewill*, there are several suicides in town. People start suspecting one student because the sculptures he makes in shop class keep appearing at the scene of the crime.

Mackall, Dandi Daley. 2003. *Kyra's Story* (Degrees of Guilt series). Wheaton, IL: Tyndale House.
A high school student has died. All his friends believe that they are partly guilty. The Degrees of Guilt trilogy, each book written by a different author, shows the perspectives of three of the friends, and why each student thinks he or she was responsible for their friend's death.

McCormick, Patricia. 2000. *Cut*. New York: Scholastic.
In *Cut*, a girl finds herself in a treatment center after she is found self-mutilating, or cutting herself.

Tashjian, Janet. 2004. *Vote for Larry*. New York: Henry Holt.
In *Vote for Larry*, Larry, from the book *The Gospel According to Larry*, decides to run for president even though he is only 18.

Wallace, Rich. 2003. *Losing Is Not an Option*. New York: Alfred A. Knopf.
If you like sports and you like short books, you might want to try this one. It is only 127 pages long and consists of short stories about a boy's trouble with girls and sports from junior high through high school.

## WHAT'S THE ONE PIECE OF ADVICE NO BOOKTALKER SHOULD FORGET?

Always remember to try to stay natural and relaxed and—most important—have fun! The books were written to engage and entertain, and
so should the booktalks that promote them. This can become one of the
best parts of your job.

## REFERENCES

Adams, Douglas. 1980. *The Hitchhiker's Guide to the Galaxy*. New York:
 Balantine Books.
Anderson, Laurie Halse. 1999. *Speak*. New York: Farrar Straus Giroux.
Anonymous. 1971. *Go Ask Alice*. New York: Simon Pulse.
Bissinger, H. G. 2004. *Friday Night Lights: A Town, a Team, and a
 Dream*. Cambridge, MA: Da Capo Press.
Bromann, Jennifer. 2001. *Booktalking That Works*. New York: Neal-
 Schuman.
Carlson, Richard. 2000. *Don't Sweat the Small Stuff for Teens*. New York:
 Hyperion.
Cai, Mingshui. 2002. *Multicultural Literature for Children and Young
 Adults: Reflections on Critical Issues*. Westport, CT: Greenwood.
Fastis, Stefan. 2001. *Word Freak*. Boston: Houghton Mifflin.
Fredericks, Mariah. 2004. *The True Meaning of Cleavage*. New York:
 Simon Pulse.
Halam, Ann. 2003. *Dr. Franklin's Island*. New York: Laurel Leaf.
Hautman, Pete. 2004. *Godless*. New York: Simon & Schuster.
Harris, Violet, ed. 1997. *Using Multiethnic Literature in K–8 Classrooms*.
 Norwood, MA: Christopher-Gordon.
Jackson, Donna M., and Charlie Fellenbaum. 1996. *The Bone Detectives:
 How Forensic Anthropologists Solve Crimes and Uncover Mysteries
 of the Dead*. Boston: Little, Brown.
Keizer, Garret. 2002. *God of Beer*. New York: HarperTempest.
McCafferty, Megan. 2001. *Sloppy Firsts*. New York: Crown.
Owen, Davis. 2002. *Hidden Secrets*. New York: Firefly Books.
Rennison, Louise. 2001. *On the Bright Side, I'm Now the Girlfriend of
 a Sex God: Further Confessions of Georgia Nicolson*. New York:
 HarperCollins.
Rowling, J. K. *Harry Potter and the Sorcerer's Stone*. 1997. New York:
 Arthur A. Levine.

Shales, Tom, and James Andrew Miller. 2002. *Live from New York: An Uncensored History of Saturday Night Live*. Boston: Little, Brown.

Simmons, Michael. 2003. *Pool Boy*. Broofield, CT: Roaring Brook.

Spiegelman, Art. 1993. *Maus*. New York: Random House.

Spinelli, Jerry. 2000. *Stargirl*. New York: Alfred A. Knopf.

They Might Be Giants (Musical Group). 2003. *Bed, Bed, Bed*. New York: Simon & Schuster.

Tolkien, J. R. R. 1997. *The Hobbit*. Boston: Houghton Mifflin.

Zusak, Markus. 2005. *I Am the Messenger*. New York: Alfred A. Knopf.

# Part II

# More Booktalking That Works

# Two Hundred Booktalks

Abrahams, George, and Sheila Ahlbrand. 2002. *Boy v. Girl? How Gender Shapes Who We Are, What We Want, and How We Get Along.* Minneapolis: Free Spirit Press.
Grades 7–12

What are the best and worst things about being a boy or a girl? One girl said a good thing is that she can cry whenever she wants. A boy said that guys are smarter, stronger, and faster. Do you think these are true? Who do you think participates more in the drill team? Boys or girls? The answer is girls with 80% and boys with 20%. How about vocal music? Yes, girls. Orchestra? Yes, girls. Dramatics? Girls. Band? Girls. Debate? Girls. The answers to what other people think can be found in this book *Boy v. Girl.*

---

Aiken, Clay. 2004. *Learning to Sing.* New York: Random House.
Grades 6–12

How many of you have seen the show *American Idol*? So you all know who Clay Aiken is, right? Well, now he has his own book. (Use the same opening for a book on a more current celebrity.) He talks about all the problems and glory he has had in his experience on *American Idol* and his fame afterwards. He mentions a time when a girl was so excited to come up on stage and sing with him. He was so excited that a girl took the time to memorize the words to his song and wondered if she felt the same way he would have if he had gotten the chance to sing with his favorite performer. Aiken mentions how hard he worked on the show while others partied and how Simon and others made fun of him for singing "Grease," wearing a red leather jacket, and attempting to dance. He talks about his love for his brother and his father's death. Even if you don't like Clay Aiken or *American Idol*, the stories are actually pretty interesting and he has some positive messages about not giving up and doing your best. (One boy took this one out for his mom. Use other interesting stories from the book)

---

Albom, Mitch. 2003. *The Five People You Meet in Heaven*. New York: Hyperion.
Grades 9–12

In radio or TV interviews you often hear questions like, "If you could have dinner with one person, dead or alive, who would that be?" People might answer the president, Jesus, a relative who has passed on, or their favorite movie, TV, or sports stars. (You could also ask the students who that person might be for them.) In the book *The Five People You Meet in Heaven*, Eddie has been killed in an amusement park accident, and so he gets his chance to meet someone who has died. He finds out that when you die, you get to meet five people whose lives you had affected, for the good or the bad. He meets a man who was killed because Eddie's ball went into the street during a game of baseball, someone he went to war with, and other people he either knew or had never met before.

---

Anderson, M. T. 2004. *The Game of Sunken Places*. New York: Scholastic.
Grades 5–9

How many of you play video games or online games that make you one of the players in the game, kind of like virtual reality? In *The Game of Sunken Places* a boy and his friend get an invitation to visit his uncle in an old mansion. When they arrive, the butler is instructed to take and burn their clothes. When they wake up they find that their clothes have been replaced with old fashioned–looking things, like knickerbockers. They soon find out that there is a board game in the house called the Game of Sunken Places. Once they start playing they are actually involved in a real game and there are no rules. Instead, they find trolls and other strange creatures and situations.

---

Anderson, M. T. 1997. *Thirsty*. Cambridge, MA: Candlewick Press.
Grades 8–12

If I told you that someone's braces just started popping off, he was hungry all the time, people were following him around, and he could no longer see his reflection in the water, what would you think? That's right.

He is a vampire. In *Thirsty*, it is not uncommon for vampires to be found in the neighborhood. Dead bodies are found all the time. Vampires are taken into custody and staked all the time. So Chris is a little worried when he starts to show signs that he might be becoming a vampire. Then someone approaches him to tell him he is a vampire, and he starts getting invitations to vampire parties, events, and a mission.

---

Anonymous [Beatrice Sparks]. 1971. *Go Ask Alice*. New York: Simon Pulse.
Grades 9–12

Think about someone you know who goes to school with you. Think about what that person is like—his or her personality. Now imagine that person as the exact opposite of what you just thought. In *Go Ask Alice*, Alice has few friends. She is so excited about moving because of the possibility of meeting new people, but it turns out to be just as bad. One summer she goes back to the last town she lived in and gets invited to a party. They play a game where some of the "lucky" kids get LSD slipped into their drinks. Alice is one. This starts her trip into drugs and running away and getting involved with all kinds of men and everything else that goes along with it. Most people think of this as a true story, but some question the veracity of the author's sources. Although it was originally published as an anonymous but true story, the author identified herself years later. The author, Beatrice Sparks, claims that a girl she was close to while working with troubled teens gave her her diary along with scraps of paper on which she wrote notes about her life during bad times. Still others believe the author is not being truthful and cannot locate information about her past work experience or education. (Information about author from Nilsen, 1979:109–112.)

Alternate talk:

(Ask the students to name some drugs. Tell them that Alice tried them all.)

Alternate talk:

You may have heard of the game spin the bottle. In *Go Ask Alice*, Alice plays a different game at a party where one of the "lucky" kids gets LSD slipped into his or her drink.

---

Aronson, Marc. 2003. *Witch-Hunt: Mysteries of the Salem Witch Trial.*
    New York: Atheneum Books.
Grades 6–12

"When you know someone envies you or has reason to resent you, and
you see that person stare at you and then you suddenly experience a
strange pain, don't you wonder if that person somehow managed to make
you suffer" (p. 15)? That is one of the questions asked in *Witch-Hunt*,
by Marc Aronson. If you have, or have had, similar thoughts, you might
be thinking in the same way that people did during the time of the Salem witch trials. Those who tell fortunes today in shops out of their
homes might have been considered witches back in the 1600s. But those
thought to be witches were usually those who made others' bodies move
uncontrollably or who were rumored to have flown through the air. Many
confessed because if they did, they would only have to be redeemed,
while those who refused to admit they were witches were killed. *Witch-
Hunt* also talks about the real reasons that people could have been considered witches. The accusers were compared to teenagers in the 50s
and 60s using rock music as a way of rebellion. Maybe the young women
in Salem were just trying to liven up the town a little.

Alternate talk:

(Start with fortune-telling.) In the 1600s I could have been accused of
being a witch for doing that.

---

Balliett, Blue. 2004. *Chasing Vermeer.* New York: Scholastic.
Grades 5–9

Let's say you get a letter that reads like this:

> Dear Friend, "I would like you to help in identifying a crime that is
> now centuries old. This crime has wronged one of the world's great-
> est painters . . . If you wish to help me, you will be amply rewarded
> for any risks you take. You may not show this letter to anyone. Two
> other people in the world have received this document tonight . . . If
> you show this to the authorities, you will most certainly be placing
> your life in danger . . . " (pp. 1-2).

(Paraphrase or mark the letter in the first chapter of the book so you can
read it.) So what would you do? Would you help solve the crime? Re-

port it to the police? What if a painting is missing and becomes national news—and you think you might be involved along with this letter? This is the story of *Chasing Vermeer*. Three people get such a letter and two young children become mixed up in solving the crime through books, observing others, and a mathematical game of pentominoes. You will find clues along the way that will help you figure out who has the Vermeer painting and who got those letters. There are even clues in the pictures.

Alternate talk:

(Give the students a code using the pentominoes and the chart given in the book and see if they can figure out you message. You might even use the names of three students in the class and then tell the audience that these three students will receive a letter and continue from there.)

---

Bauer, Joan. 1995. *Thwonk*. New York: Delacorte Press.
Grades 7–10

> . . . I slammed on the brakes.
> Trish sat up with a start.
> A small thing rolled out of the box. It did a kind of half somersault and landed spread eagle in front of my Volvo. "What was that?" Trish asked sleepily.
> "I don't know . . ."
> I kept the headlights on and began to get out of the car. . . .
> "*Stay in the car, A. J. It's late and something's weird!*"
> I peered over the dashboard, turned on my brights.
> "Maybe you killed it," Trish offered.
> I got out, walked to the front of the car, my heart racing. I took one look at the thing in the street.
> "*Please,*" I said, giggling.
> Trish was huddled in the car, motioning me to come back. I knelt down to get a better look. My headlights shone a yellow glow across the figure.
> "What is it?" Trish shouted.
> I laughed out loud.
> It was a dilapidated cupid doll as big as my hand with a battered bow-and-arrow and a stupid grin.
> I picked it up.
> But maybe she shouldn't have and maybe it wasn't a doll.

(This section can be found on pages 39–40 in *Thwonk*.)

Alternate talk:

Let's say that you are out driving your car, or your parents are driving if you don't drive yet, and you hit something. You get out and take a look. It's not an animal or a person, but it is moving and it has an arrow. Now I know it is unlikely, but it is Cupid. Cupid will do one thing for you. He doesn't only shoot someone with his arrow to make him or her fall in love with you. He could help your career or do anything else. He says he isn't that great at teen relationships. He has screwed up before. Would you take love or help with your future career or school? (Wait for responses.) In *Thwonk*, this actually does happen to A. J. and she is so in love with Peter that she doesn't listen to Cupid's advice and goes for love. Only it doesn't work out as perfectly as she had hoped.

Bauer, Marion Dane, ed. 1994. *Am I Blue?* New York: HarperCollins
Grades 9–12

You have probably heard of the term "gaydar" before. That is the ability for a person to detect when someone is gay or lesbian. Well, *Am I Blue?* is a collection of short stories about teenagers who are gay or who know people who are gay. In the first story, a boy comes across his fairy godfather, who offers him three wishes. The boy decides to use his last wish to make every person in the world know for just one day who is gay and who is not gay by making those who are gay turn blue. Now some people will have more blue than others. Those with just a little blue might not be sure or might not be ready to come out yet. In another story, a teenager learns a friend has AIDS, and in another a girl must make the decision to come out to her parents.

Alternate talk:

If you had three wishes, what would you wish for? Well, in *Am I Blue?* . . .

Behrendt, Greg, and Liz Tuccillo. 2004. *He's Just Not That into You*. New York: Simon & Schuster.
Grades 11–12

This is a book for the girls in the room. So maybe you are dating this guy and he keeps apologizing for not calling because he has basketball practice and a job and homework and his parents made him clean the yard. Well, guess what? He's just not that into you. He could have used his cell phone while raking leaves or on his way to work. Okay. So maybe you know this guy who always calls you. He tells you everything. He asks what you are doing on the weekend, but he never asks you out! Your friends say he is just shy. Guess what? He's just not that into you. So you meet a guy at a party who goes to a different school. You talk for hours, but he doesn't ask for your number. You wonder if you should try to call a friend who knows his friend to find his number. Guess what? He's just not that into you. If he really wanted to, he could find your number. He knows the friend who knows your friend. I could go on forever, but the authors of this book, who were writers for the television show *Sex and the City*, pretty much say that if a guy likes you he will find time for you. If he really likes you he will ask you out or find where you are. But don't be too quick to take the advice, since it is coming from a man who writes for TV and has no degree in psychology.

---

Bennett, James. 1995. *The Squared Circle*. New York: Scholastic.
Grades 9–12

You have probably heard of incidents in college sports in which players have been paid to sign. The school wants them to play on their team so badly that they throw them parties or give them money or cars or set them up with a place to live—or even give them passing grades. In *The Squared Circle*, Sonny has chosen to take the basketball scholarship at Southern Illinois University, which was partly his uncle's choice. There is an NCAA investigation going on at his school, and he continues to be interviewed. He is asked things like, "Does your uncle give you money?" and "Who do you give your family tickets to?" He never questioned any of this before, but he did get a rather nice car from his uncle as an early birthday present. Sonny soon starts to question these investigations himself and wonders how he really ended up at SIU.

---

Bloor, Edward. 1997. *Tangerine*. New York: Scholastic.
Grades 5–9

You may have some family secrets that you have to keep hidden. In *Tangerine* by Edward Bloor, Paul's family has a secret. Paul is practically blind. They tell him this is so because he once stared at the sun too long. His family moves to a new home in Florida. His brother is the football star and Paul's game is soccer. When they find out that Paul is legally blind without his glasses, the school no longer wants him to be the goalie because of possible liability. Paul switches schools to one that is much rougher than his last one and joins the soccer team there without telling anyone about his condition. But there is still the family secret of why Paul has to wear these glasses and why he can't see without them.

Boyce, Frank Cottrell. 2004. *Millions*. New York: HarperCollins.
Grades 4–8

Raise your hand if you found $20 on the street and you'd keep it. Raise your hand if you'd keep it if you found it at school. Even if it was right under your friend's desk? Raise your hand if you'd keep a bag you found with a million dollars in it. Raise your hand if you'd tell anyone. What if you heard on the news that there was a robbery and the thieves had thrown some money exactly where you found it? Raise your hand if you'd still keep the money. Raise your hand if you would admit you had the money if the police came to your door to ask about it. Now if you would keep it, what would you do with all that money so no one would suspect you had it, even though your house is right where it was supposed to have been left? What if you only had a certain amount of time to spend it because your country's currency was about to change? These are questions that two brothers have to decide in the book *Millions*. They don't tell their father, and they start by paying kids at school for their lunches and toys. Then they move on to bigger things. (You might also want to mention that the author writes screenplays for movies, including this one, although most students will not have heard of them.)

Brashares, Ann. 2001. *The Sisterhood of the Traveling Pants*. New York: Delacorte Press
Grades 6–12

Think about your friends or look at the people around you. Do you think you could fit into their jeans? Borrow their clothes? Probably not. Everyone is a different size. In *The Sisterhood of the Traveling Pants*, four friends find a pair of jeans in a thrift store. They find one pair that everyone loves. They each try them on to see which of them best fits into these fabulous jeans. Amazingly, that one pair of pants fits each one of them and they are all different sizes. One is thin, one has a self-proclaimed big butt, another is short, and another is tall. They decide that these jeans have to be magic. The problem is that each of them will be in a different part of the country or world this summer. So they decide to take turns with the pants and mail them back and forth to each other to hopefully solve all their problems with boys, family, and their lives. The girls continue their adventures in *The Second Summer of the Sisterhood*.

Alternate talk:

You probably would not be able to fit into most of your friends' clothes. (Then use plot summary.)

---

Bridges, Ruby. 1999. *Through My Eyes*. New York: Scholastic. Grades 4–8

Anyone who lives in this town can go to this school. But in the 1960s there were still segregated schools. Black children were not allowed to go to school with white children, even though the United States government said they could. In 1960, Louisiana allowed some black children to go to white schools if they passed a test. Only a few passed this difficult test, and Ruby Bridges was going to be the only black student at her school. It turned out that she was the only student at her school. Most parents still did not want a black child in their school, and the protesters scared others away. Some threw things at Ruby. Some had signs and shouted out hateful things, and one had a coffin with a black doll in it. *Through My Eyes* is told by Ruby Bridges. Others have written about her before, but now she tells her own story of what she remembers and how life was for her after being one of the first children to integrate schools in the south. (Use with *Yankee Girl* by Mary Rodman.)

---

Bronson, Jeremy. 2002. *What Animal Are You?* Boulder, CO: SPS Studios. Grades 7–12

If you could be any animal, what would you be? Well, that may be the animal you think you are, but the book *What Animal Are You?* will ask questions to test your personality and tell you what animal you really are and why you might be, say, a chuckwalla, who likes to be near home, or an oxpecker, who is gossipy and social, or a leech, who keeps friends for a long time, or a wild rat, who gets what he wants. (Select other examples from the book.)

---

Bruchac, Joseph. *Skeleton Man*. 2001. New York: HarperCollins.
Grades 4–9

(Tell the story from the beginning of this book.) There is a Native American legend that says there was once an uncle who invited his family over for dinner. While cooking the meal, he burned himself. He went to lick his finger (lick your finger) and he thought, "This tastes good." So he eats his finger. But he is still hungry and he wants more, so he eats his other fingers. Then he eats his toes and his arms and his legs until he is just a skeleton man. That is a Mohawk Indian story, but, in the book *Skeleton Man* by Joseph Bruchac, it really happens. One day a young girl's parents don't come home. After a couple days she decides to go back to school, knowing her parents will return. They never do, but a strange skeletal-looking man comes to school claiming to be her uncle. He locks her in her room and seems to poison her food, and she has to find a way to locate her parents and get away from this strange man.

---

Burgess, Melvin. 1998. *Smack*. New York: Holt.
Grades 9–12

"The title is exactly what you think it is. Heroin. A group of teenagers who are living in some abandoned houses use what is left of their minds and bodies to get it" (Bromann, 1999).

Alternate talk:

(Ask what "smack" means, or ask for other words for it or for other drugs.)

---

Butler, Robert Olen. 2004. *Had a Good Time: Stories from American Postcards*. New York: Grove Press.
Grades 9–12.

(Show the students a postcard on an overhead or PowerPoint, or just read one to them.) Now what do you think really happened to this person? (Ask questions related to the card.) Did that person ever come home? Did something happen along the way? Robert Olen Butler collected postcards from way back to the early 1900s. He read the postcards, read newspaper articles about events occurring during that time, and then wrote short stories about what he thought really happened to the people who sent those cards. One such card read:

Dear Pauline, Arrived at Portland yesterday morning and it was such a relieve for we had an upper berth and I didn't sleep a wink. Well I got married to Milk Can and we are now on our honey moon. Mr. Watt is here and he looks stunning, Katie (p. 163).

You may have your own idea about what happened to Katie, but Robert Olen Butler has his. In his story called "I Got Married to Milk Can," the author decides to marry Katie to a milk farmer. On their trip she runs across a former love interest and artist, Mr. Watt. He wants to take her away to the artist's life of future luxury. Although the life of a dairy farmer's wife is not extravagant and Mr. Watt is much more handsome than her husband—who no one knows she calls Milk Can but her friends—she runs off to stay with her new husband. This is one of the many stories based on postcards in *Had a Good Time*.

Alternate talk:

(Start by reading a postcard from the book and asking the students what happened. Then tell them Butler's version.)

---

Cabot, Meg. 2004. *The Mediator 6: Twilight*. New York: HarperCollins. Grades 7–12

Have any of you ever seen those shows about people who talk to the dead, like *Crossing Over* with John Edward? How many of you believe it is real and that he and others can really contact the dead? How many of you believe it is a trick? There was actually an episode of Dateline on which they tried to prove whether John Edward was a fraud or he really could communicate with the dead. Even some celebrities believed he could. But when he said he was hearing from someone from the past of one of the cameramen, it was later shown that Edward had talked to the cameraman before the show. The Mediator series by Meg Cabot, who wrote the Princess Diaries series, is about a mediator or a shifter or someone who can communicate with the dead. The deceased contact them for help. In this series, Suze wants to help them and tries. She has even fallen in love with one of the ghosts, Jesse. But her friend Paul is also a mediator, and he uses the gift to help himself. He likes Suze, so he wants to go back in time to stop her ghost boyfriend from being murdered so he won't talk to Suze in the future. And when a dead woman asks for help in showing her family where her hidden money is, he takes it for himself. Suze has to stop this from happening. There are six books in this series, and you don't necessarily have to start with the first one, although it would help you better understand their gift and how it happened. (You can use this type of booktalk for any of the books in the series.)

Alternate talk:

Many of you have probably had trouble finding a boyfriend or girlfriend who will always be there for you. Maybe he doesn't call when he says he will, or he decides to go out with his friends and blows you off. Well, for Suze in the Mediator series, her problem is different. Her boyfriend is a ghost.

---

Cabot, Meg. 2004. *Teen Idol.* New York: HarperCollins.
Grades 7–10

Think of a movie or TV star whom you would love to meet. (You can ask for names if you'd like.) In the book *Teen Idol*, a girl gets her chance. Jen is trusted with the job of being the school newspaper's advice columnist. Since she has to keep her identity a secret, she is also trusted to keep the secret, even from her friends, that a movie star is coming to their school undercover to research his next role. This book is by the author of the Princess Diary series.

Alternate talk.

You know those advice columns in newspapers and magazines. Well, Jen . . .

---

Carlson, Richard. 2000. *Don't Sweat the Small Stuff for Teens.* New York: Hyperion.
Grades 5–12

Think of all the celebrities you know who have been married multiple times or who have had multiple relationships. Let's name some. (Give suggestions of people popular at the time.) Winona Ryder dates band guys like the guy from Soul Asylum. She has been out with Matt Damon and Johnny Depp. J Lo was on her third or fourth marriage and she dated P Diddy and Ben Affleck. They call her a serial wife. Gwyneth Paltrow has been with Brad Pitt and Ben Affleck and others. Drew Barrymore has been married twice already and is always dating. (Use current examples.) So if these people who can get almost anyone they want have had multiple relationships, why should anyone be upset over a break up? #3 in *Don't Sweat the Small Stuff for Teens* is titled "Don't Sweat the Breakups" (pp. 12–13). A point that it makes is that almost no one ever marries his or her first date and rarely his or her first love. It is hard to lose someone you love, but know that there will be others—just as there are for celebrities.

Alternate talk:

#12 "Let Him Have His Accident Somewhere Else" (pp. 34–35). (Ask the group what they would do if someone was tailgating them. Repeat this phrase.)

#34 "Avoid the 90–10 Trap" (pp. 89–91). (Ask students to think about everything that happened to them today and what they were most worried about. Point out all the things that went well and discuss how we dwell on the negative and give less credit to the positive things, which probably occur more often throughout the day.)

#48 "Read a Minimum of Eight Pages a Day" (pp. 122–123). If you do you will have read 30,000 pages in 10 years. If an average book is 300 pages, that is 100 books you otherwise would have not read.

#61 "Dish Out Praise" (pp. 150–152). (Ask teens what qualities people they like have. If they say they are nice or complimentary, tell them that people who are well liked tend to be people who compliment you and perhaps you should do the same to others.)

#64 "Use Reminder Cards" (pp. 157–158). (Give each student a card. They can have phrases suggested in this chapter or titles of each section in the book or ideas you write on your own. Tell students about the idea of carrying around a card of affirmations they come across as a reminder. How often do we hear a quote from Oprah or Dr. Phil or from a book we read or from a teacher, and we live by it one day and forget it the next. If you write them down you will never forget. Use a variety of the above possibilities or just one. Select the best one for the age group you work with.)

Carroll, Andrew, ed. 2002. *War Letters: Extraordinary Correspondence from American Wars.* New York: Washington Square Press.
Grades 9–12

On television and in books you can see pictures of war, but you don't often get to hear what people really thought or felt during war time. *War Letters* is a collection of letters gathered by Andrew Carroll. He asked people to send him letters and got over 50,000. He includes some from the Civil War, WWI, WWII, the Vietnam War, Desert Storm, and Somalia/Bosnia/Kosovo in this book. There is one letter about a boy who pretended to be older than he was to be allowed to fight at war. But when things got too hard and he wanted to go home, his mother conveniently could not locate his identification. Another man married right before he went to war, but met another woman while he was away. Fortunately, his first wife was understanding when he returned home.

Carvell, Marlene. 2002. *Who Will Tell My Brother?* New York: Hyperion.
Grades 7–12

(Find out the name of the school's mascot if you do not know what it is. Say something similar to what follows.) Your school's mascot is a bulldog. Maybe you have a student dressed as a dog to prance around on the field or court or you have a barking chant. In some schools, though, the mascot is an Indian. A student might dress up as an Indian and cheerleaders might wear feathers in their hair. Hundreds, if not thousands, of schools still have Native Americans as their school's mascot. However, more than 600 schools and colleges have changed this mascot (from the note at the end of the book). This is the story of a Native American boy who is offended and tries to get his high school to stop using an Indian as the school's symbol of pride. People call him names and try to attack him along the way. It is based on the true story of what happened to this author's two sons during high school. (You might also choose to read from the book since it is in verse. The section headed "September 28: School Spirit" deals with Evan's experience as an Indian is used as a mascot during an assembly [p. 12]).

Chatzky, Jean. 2004. *Pay It Down!* New York: Penguin.
Grades 11–12

You probably have no interest in saving money for a house, and you probably don't have any debt to pay off right now. So you probably don't need this book. However, if you do want a house someday and you do want to stay out of debt, you might want to take a look at this book. *Pay It Down* is written by a woman who often appears on *The Today Show*. She offers advice on how to stay out of debt and how to save money by putting away just ten dollars a day. She talks about how your credit score is determined, which is what creditors use to give you loans or credit cards. She talks about how to create a budget and how long it will take to pay off debt. So, even if you don't really need this now, it might be something you want to start thinking about for the future.

Childs, T. Mike. 2004. *The Rocklopedia Fakebandica*. New York: St. Martin's Griffin.
Grades 7–12

Have you ever heard of the band Krusty and the Krums? (They may know it is from *The Simpsons*. Then ask them to name the TV shows or movies the bands listed here were in. If no one says *The Simpsons* continue to ask if they know the other bands.) How about The Larry Davis Experience? Yes. Also from *The Simpsons*. Leather and the Suedes? *Happy Days*. Remember that one from reruns? The Libby Chessler Generation? *Sabrina the Teenage Witch*. Maggot Death? *The School of Rock*. The Max Rebo Band? *Return of the Jedi*. Moop? *South Park*. Jimmy Moore? *The Wedding Singer*. Phlegm? *The Brady Bunch Movie*. The Pinheads? *Back to the Future*. The Soggy Bottom Boys? *O Brother Where Art Thou*. Vanilla Lice? *Tiny Toon Adventures*. The Bikini Bottom Super Band? *Spongebob Squarepants*. Johnny Bravo? *The Brady Bunch*. Well, all of these are fake bands that have appeared in TV shows or movies. You can find them all listed in the *Rocklopedia Fakebandica* along with information about how they appeared in the shows. (Select the bands from the book you think your students are most likely to recognize.)

Clarke, Miranda. 2003. *Night of a Thousand Boyfriends*. Philadelphia: Quirk Books.
Grades 11–12

How many of you used to read those Choose Your Own Adventure books when you were younger? Or maybe still read them? Or maybe you took one of those quizzes in a teen magazine where you have to jump to certain squares depending on whether you would tell your friends' secrets or get in trouble yourself. This is the concept of the book *Night of a Thousand Boyfriends*. In the story you are the girl (sorry guys, you probably won't want to be reading this one), and you get to decide how you want your date to go. Now, don't tell your teacher, but this book probably took me less than 10 minutes to read, even though it is over 100 pages, because I guess I screwed up my date by talking too much about my ex-boyfriend. I know they say never to do that, but I didn't like the other choices. So why don't you take a look at this book and see if you can get a better date. (Your talk may change depending on the outcome of your story).

Cobb, Katie. 2002. *Happenings*. New York: HarperTrophy.
Grades 6–10

Would you like it if (insert the name of the teacher for whom you are booktalking) just stopped teaching and you didn't have to listen in class anymore? (Most answers will be "Yes.") Well, what if you needed to know the material so you could get a good score on your ACT (or other test)? What if instead of teaching you, he or she just gave you worksheets? Would you like that any better? Well, that is what happens to Kelsey at her school. Her teacher just stops teaching and the class is incredibly bored. You think you have it bad. Maybe you can't imagine how boring it would be to do worksheets every single day in class and for homework. Her class is so upset that they protest by refusing to do homework or refusing to leave the class. Instead, they just sit there. You might think this would be great, but their families ground them and, worse, they might not graduate.

Colfer, Eoin. 2004. *The Supernaturalist*. New York: Hyperion.
Grades 6–10

*The Supernaturalist* is about a boy in the future who happens to live in an orphanage. Only orphanages are a little different in the future. Here they use the children in human experiments to make money. One boy really wants to escape, except they can track the children by the chemicals in their pores which is given to them when they take showers. But one day he gets his chance. There is break in the system where he can't be detected. But now he has to deal with toxic rain and people who want to stop him—until he meets the Supernaturalist.

Cooney, Caroline B. 1994. *Driver's Ed*. New York: Delacorte Press.
Grades 7–12

You might have heard in the news, a few years back, a story about some teenagers who took down a stop sign just for fun. It was on one of those news-magazine shows like *Dateline*. Well, at the intersection where they removed the sign, that night a car went through just as a truck was going by and it killed the passengers in the car. The case may have been appealed, but the teenagers were originally sentenced to do time for their responsibility in this crime. A few years earlier, Caroline Cooney wrote about the same thing in *Driver's Ed*, only they get off a little easier in the story than in real life. (Adapted from Bromann, 1999:63.)

Cooney, Caroline. 1990. *The Face on the Milk Carton*. New York: Bantam.
Grades 6–11

A couple of years ago (you might say 2003 or _____ years ago, depending on when you present the booktalk) a boy was surfing the Web at school and came across a missing-children's Web site. He found a picture of himself. He soon found out that his father had had custody of him, but his mother abducted him 14 years earlier. The author Caroline Cooney must predict the future, because she writes about almost the same thing in her book *The Face on the Milk Carton*. One day a girl is sitting at lunch and sees her own picture on a milk carton. She didn't know that she was missing, so she has to try to find out why someone else thinks she is.

Cormier, Robert. 2001. *The Rag and Bone Shop*. New York: Delacorte Press.
Grades 6–10

(Walk up to a student. Use one who has been pretending to not pay attention or enjoy your talks.) You stole my pencil. (He or she will deny it.) I just had it at my desk. I saw you over there. And now it is gone. Don't tell me you didn't take it. (Luckily for you, most students will then pretend to agree with you that they took it.) That is exactly what happens to Jason in *The Rag and Bone Shop*. A seven-year-old girl he knows from his neighborhood has been murdered and the police question him about it, trying to get out of him if he is the one who killed her.

---

Cormier, Robert. 1997. *Tenderness*. New York: Delacorte Press.
Grades 8–12

Who are some of your favorite actors, sports stars, singers? You might have some of their pictures in your locker or on the wall in your room. Perhaps you have memorized all their songs or stats. But I doubt you're going to run away and track them down and follow them. In *Tenderness* by Robert Cormier, Lori does just that. Only her idol is a serial killer (Adapted from Bromann, 1999:63).

---

Corrigan, Eireann. 2002. *You Remind Me of You*. New York: Scholastic.
Grades 9–12

One day Eireann Corrigan finds her boyfriend with a gun in his hand, ready to commit suicide. She writes in poems about this and her experience with eating disorders.

---

Coville, Bruce, and Jane Yolen. 1998. *Armageddon Summer*. New York: Harcourt Brace.
Grades 7–8

Maybe your parents force you to go to church or to your aunt's house or shopping with them, but at least they don't take you to the top of a mountain to camp behind a closed-in fence with armed guards because they are convinced the world is going to end. In *Armageddon Summer*, Marina and Jed take turns telling the story of what happened on that mountain. (Younger audiences might appreciate the fact that each author took on a different character's voice like in *P.S. Longer Letter Later* by Paula Danziger and Ann M. Martin.)

---

Creech, Sharon. 2004. *Heartbeat*. New York: HarperCollins. Grades 4–8

What do you love more than anything else? (This is a question from the teacher in the book along with "What do you fear most?") Do you like to run? In *Heartbeat* by Sharon Creech, Annie loves to run, especially with her friend Max. She doesn't love that the track coach is trying to get her to join the team because she just wants to run for herself and not for competition. She loves her grandfather who is living with her and her mother who is about to have a baby, and she is not sure how much she loves her friend Max. The book is written in poetry form although it doesn't sound like poems and should only take you about an hour to read.

---

Creech, Sharon. 2001. *Love That Dog*. New York: Scholastic. Grades 3–9

What is your favorite poem? (Wait for answers.) Here is mine. (Read one of your favorite poems.) Jack's favorite poems are by Walter Dean Myers. In *Love That Dog*, he has to write a journal about poetry for his teacher so he writes about *his* dog and finds out that he might actually be a poet. And he also gets a chance to meet his favorite author.

Alternate talk:

(Ask students to identify some of the poems in the book *Love That Dog*.)

Alternate talk:

(Ask students to help you write a poem about a dog. Then share one of Jack's poems about his dog from the book.)

Crespo, Clare. 2002. *The Secret Life of Food*. New York: Hyperion.
Grades 4–12

How many of you like to cook? How many of you can cook? Okay, how many of you just like to play with your food? Did any of you make any strange creations when you were a kid, or maybe yesterday? *The Secret Life of Food* gives you the chance to play with your food but also to create something edible. (Show pictures from the book.) For example, you can make a football meatloaf, a Jell-O egg, eyeballs, spaghetti with eyeballs, or handwiches.

Alternate talk:

(Make some of the food from the book and bring it to show.)

Curtis, Christopher Paul. 1995. *The Watsons Go to Birmingham–1963*.
     New York: Dell Laurel-Leaf.
Grades 4–9

Raise your hand if your family has an eight-track player in their car? A radio? A cassette player? CD player? Satellite radio? Well, in *The Watson's Go to Birmingham*, the father of two boys gets their car ready for a road trip by installing a record player in their car, called the Ultra Glide. They are going on a trip to Birmingham because their oldest son keeps getting into trouble and his punishment, or the way to try to reform him, is to send him to his grandmother's place in another state. He uses store credit to buy cookies when they hardly have money to eat, and he is constantly causing problems. They drive straight through only to get to a city where there are lots of racial issues and bombings of churches.

Daltow, Ellen, ed. 2003. *The Dark: New Ghost Stories*. New York: Tom Doherty.
Grades 10–12

There was a woman who was recently divorced because she just couldn't live with her husband anymore after her son died. It was her fault he died. It was an accident, but she blamed herself. She knew she was responsible. And now her son, husband, and even her cat are gone. One night she is lying in bed and feels something on her leg. She hears a scratching noise and a thud on the floor. She turns the lights on, only no one and nothing is there. The door is closed. Then she goes to the kitchen. Everything above the countertops is fine, but everything below is a mess. It is like an animal or child got into everything. There are claw marks on the cabinets, the garbage can is knocked over and has spilled everywhere, and there are even feces and blood. She calls her ex-husband over. He stays. He thinks they are getting back together but the next day she tells him they are not. The next night she hears noises again. This time she hears talking. She calls her ex-husband but this time he refuses to come. That was just one of the ghost stories in *The Dark*.

DeMille, Nelson. 2004. *Night Fall*. New York: Warner Books.
Grades 10–12

You may be too young to remember, but on July 17, 1996, TWA flight 800 exploded in the sky off the coast of Long Island killing over 200 people bound for Paris. The official report is that it went down because of an explosion in the center fuel tank. But there are many other theories. One major theory that is supported by 200 witnesses is that a missile shot down this plane. Many people saw a streak of light go up from the water rather than down from the plane, as the government suggests. So what if the conspiracy theories are right? The author Nelson DeMille takes some actual people and the actual events of the TWA flight 800 case and turns it into fiction. It begins with a couple who are having an affair. They capture the plane crash on tape but want no one else to see what else is on that tape besides the crash, so they erase it. Detective John Corey knows there is more to this case and sets out to find answers and the witnesses who never got a chance to testify. But people are following him. People want him off this case. People want him dead. So even though this book is almost 500 pages long, it is like you are reading a movie script, and you will want to get to the shocking end. Still today many people think that it was not a fuel tank explosion but a missile fired at the plane. You can decide what you think after reading this book and checking the Internet for Web sites about the crash.

DeVillers, Julia. 2004. *How My Private, Personal Journal Became a Bestseller*. New York: Dutton.
Grades 5–10

How many of you have had to write a journal for one of your classes before? Did anyone ever have a teacher who read that journal out loud to the class? (You could also begin with one or more of the "magazine" questions that begin each chapter, such as "Would you take off your clothes and run around the school in your underwear for $1,000? $3,000? $5,000?") Well, you might want to hold onto your next journal assignment because in *How My Private, Personal Journal Became a Bestseller*, a girl's journal is not only read in class, but it is submitted to a publisher and she instantly becomes a rich celebrity.

---

DeVillers, Julia. 2002. *GirlWise: How to Be Confident, Capable, Cool, and in Control*. Roseville, CA: Prima.
Grades 6–12

Here is a tip if you have ever been at a party or anywhere where you find yourself by yourself with no one to talk to. Pick up your cell phone and pretend to be having a conversation with someone. (Use your hand or a cell phone to demonstrate talking on a phone.) That way no one will think you are by yourself; everyone will assume you left to answer a call. In fact, why not make up a witty conversation to get others interested in talking to you. That is just one suggestion from *GirlWise*.

Alternate talk:

(Ask students, "Who is your best friend?" Tell them they are wrong. Tell them their best friends are themselves. Ask students something special they would do for a date or someone they liked. Where would you take them? What would you give them? What would you say to them? Take the suggestion from the book and tell students to date themselves. This will surely get laughs, but you'll get their attention. Tell them that whatever they would do for a date or someone they like, they should do for themselves. If they would buy a date flowers, they should buy themselves flowers. If they would take a date to a movie, then they should take themselves to a movie.)

Alternate talk:

(Ask the students to think of celebrities they admire. Ask for a volunteer to come up and show how that person would act. You might have two or three do a scene together. The book suggests that to feel confident about getting a guy you should "pretend you are a celebrity whom everyone adores" (p. 16). Tell them this is one of the ways they can look confident. Remind them they don't actually have to dress or walk or talk like the celebrity, but they should think like the celebrity. )

Alternate Talk:

(If you want a silly opening, ask a volunteer to act out how a confident person acts and walks as described on page 16, such as "Stand tall with your shoulders back," "Hold your head high," "Smile," "Look people in the eye," "Keep your hands away from your clothing," "Stand firm," and "Sit tall." Use one or combine the suggestions above.)

---

Draper, Sharon M. 1999. *Romiette and Julio.* New York: Atheneum Books.
   Grades 7–12

Your best friend tells you she just met a guy on the Internet. What advice would you give her? (Wait for advice or mention what people usually say.) And that is almost exactly what Destiny, Romiette's best friend, tells her. Only she gets a little more freaked out by it. She says stuff like:

> "Girl, that's where serial killers and rapists be hanging out. They make you think they're okay, then they make plans to meet you then you end up with your picture on the back of a milk carton! Those sex stalkers on the Internet know exactly what to say to make you think they're the same age as you are . . . You're gonna get raped and mutilated and I don't have a thing to wear to your funeral! . . . You didn't tell him, did you? Your shoe size or your breast size! . . . You know, Romi, those kinds of people can trace you. They have secret codes they put in their computer and then they figure out where your phone line is hooked up and then they come to your house and ring your doorbell and slice your heart out after they have sex with you . . . Anyone with a screen name like Spanishlover is up to no good. I saw a talk show where this one man was giving these girls this drug called Spanish fly. He would drug them, and they wouldn't

know if the man was having sex with them or not, and he got them all pregnant . . . I saw another talk show where they used these private chat rooms to bug the phone lines of the people they lured into them. Then they stole their identities and charged up millions of dollars on their credit cards" (pp. 51–54).

But Romiette is really safe in this situation. At least safe from her online boyfriend, that is. He actually happens to be a new guy at her school. The only trouble she has to worry about is the people who don't like that she, a black girl, is dating a Hispanic man. If you haven't figured it out, *Romiette and Julio* is almost like *Romeo and Juliet*, and I am not going to tell you if they end up dying for each other like in Shakespeare's story.

---

Druckman, Nancy. 2003. *American Flags: Designs for a Young Nation.* New York: Harry N. Abrams.
Grades 6–12

Does anyone know why the canton, or blue box with the stars, on the American flag usually rests on a white stripe but sometimes on a red one? Any guesses? Some flag collectors believe that when a canton rests on a red stripe it was made during wartime to represent the blood shed by soldiers. This is just one of the many facts about the history of the United States flag that can be found in the book *American Flags*. In this book, you learn you can determine the age of a flag by the number of stars representing the number of states in the union and more than you ever wanted to know about homemade United States flags.

Alternate talk:

(Show flags with different numbers of stars and see if the students can determine what year they were adopted or which state(s) entered the union that year.)

---

Edut, Tali and Ophira. 2003. *Astro Style: Star-Studded Advice for Love, Life, and Looking Good.* New York: Simon & Schuster.
Grades 7–12

(Approach or point to a student.) What's your sign? (Have the pages marked for the astrological signs in your book.) So, you are a Virgo. Let's see if this book is right. For a gift you might want a photo album/storage box, manicure/electric shaver, desk lamp, journal, clothes that are earthy or white, a health club membership, drinking glasses, or a laptop. Am I right? Well, right or not, if your friends read this book that is what they are going to give you. Okay. Let's try someone else. What's your sign? Leo? Think of someone you like. What is his sign? Capricorn? Okay. Let's see if you are compatible. You like this person simply on the basis of how you both look together, right? It seems this Capricorn guy might leave you attention-starved and neglected. So watch for that. In *Astro Style* you can learn about yourself and your friends' relationships and life simply by your astrological sign.

---

Efaw, Amy. 2000. *Battle Dress.* New York: HarperCollins.
Grades 9–12

Years ago a girl named Shannon Faulkner fought the Supreme Court to be admitted to an all-boys' military academy, the Citadel. After she was admitted, she found it tougher than she had expected, and she only lasted about a week. However, now women can be admitted, and they do make it through and graduate. *Battle Dress* is a fictional story of a similar event. A girl wants to go to West Point with the other young men and women, but she finds it a little tougher than expected, with drills in the cold night, cruel treatment from the upper classmen, and the endless exercises. It is far worse than her miserable home life.

---

Ehrenhart, Daniel. 2004. *10 Things to Do before I Die.* New York: Delacorte Press.
Grades 9–12

If you found out that you only had 24 hours to live, what would you want to do with that time? (If no one answers, ask questions like, "Would you go to school?" "Would you tell a girl you like her?" "Would you go somewhere?") In *10 Things to Do before I Die*, Ted finds out that the french fries he was eating at a local restaurant were poisoned and he only has 24 hours to live. His friends had been making up a list of things he needed to accomplish, and now he only has a day to finish them. So this starts his adventure of trying to get to another country, of trying to be a hero, and trying to play with his favorite band, Shakes the Clown. He causes a lot of trouble, but he is dying so he can't get in trouble for it, or maybe he can.

Esquivel, Laura. 1992. *Like Water for Chocolate*. New York: Doubleday.
Grades 9–12

Here's a question for the guys in the room, but the girls can answer too. Let's say there is someone you really like and you've been dating her for a long time—like a week. You decide it is time to go meet the parents. Or maybe she decides for you. You go in your closet and into the hamper and find a shirt that smells okay, pull on your best pair of ripped jeans, and head over to the house. Only when the parents open the door, they practically scream when they see you. They can smell you, they see the holes in your clothes in all the wrong places and the earrings in your ear, and then they look at your car. It has a door missing—on the passenger side—the mirrors are taped on, the bumper is hanging off, and there is what looks to be a bullet hole in the windshield. There is no way they are letting you out with their daughter. You can't see her anymore. You can't talk to her in school. You can't e-mail her. You can't call her on the phone. So what are you going to do to find a way to be with this girl? (Wait for answers.) Well, that is not what Pedro did in *Like Water for Chocolate*. In this book, Tita is not allowed to marry Pedro because the strong Mexican tradition says that the youngest in the family has to take care of the mother for as long as she is alive. So Pedro has a great idea. Instead of doing all the things you have suggested, he decides to go and marry Tita's sister so at least they can live in the house together. Definitely not the smartest idea, but that's what they did. Tita's cooking is so magical that it has an effect on the people who eat it. After Tita cries into the cake she makes for her sister's wedding, everyone who eats the cake feels an overwhelming sadness and cries. After she is upset she cannot be with Pedro and is angry while cooking food for her sister, her sister suddenly gets ill and has really bad breath. This was also made into a movie and since the movie has subtitles it is actually like you are reading the book anyway. (Adapted from Bromann, 1999:61–62).

---

Evans, Richard Paul. 1995. *The Christmas Box*. New York: Simon & Schuster.
Grades 8–12

Even though it is not Christmas, you still might enjoy this really short book that will take you about an hour to read; it is called *The Christmas Box*. This story was originally self-published and only meant to be read by the author's children. But it was soon discovered and became a bestseller. It is about a couple and their child who move into the house of an older woman to help care for her while living rent-free. While living there, the husband uncovers a box of old letters revealing secrets about the woman.

---

Farmer, Nancy. 2002. *The House of the Scorpion*. Atheneum.
Grades: 5–12

What do you think the age of the oldest living person is? Well, it is hard to say because often people in other countries have no written proof of their age. It may be 119, 124, or even 129. But this is not rare in *The House of the Scorpions*. In this futuristic novel, people can live to be over 140 years old. They may never die because they have mastered cloning. People are cloned in order to use the body parts to save the original person. When the clones are born, their minds are destroyed so that they are really not good for much except their body parts. Other people have something implanted in their heads so that they continue to do the same task without stopping unless they are told to do so. One clone has survived this fate. His father is powerful so he is able to request his clone's mind not be destroyed. The boy is kept in the house of a maid until he is discovered. Some people think of clones as nothing but animals. Others see them as real people. So Matt is safe for now, until he escapes.

Alternate talk:

You might have heard stories about people selling their organs for money so that other people can live. Or stories about people having babies just so they can use the bone marrow for another child to survive. This is controversial. But this is real in the futuristic book *The House of Scorpions*.

---

Fastis, Stefan. 2001. *Word Freak*. Boston: Houghton Mifflin.
Grades 9–12

(Have a bag or box full of Scrabble™ letters. Ask seven students to pick out a letter. Write them on a board or on paper on the wall or ask students to keep track.) Now how many words can you make with these letters? (Ask for some words created.) This is just one of the many activities professional Scrabble™ players use to practice. And yes, some people make a living trying to win Scrabble™ tournaments. Stefan Fastis decided to enter their world and he followed some players around and attended Scrabble™ tournaments to find out how they know so much and why they love it so much. He even started to play himself. So one thing he discovered was that players take long words and see how many smaller words they can make from them. Sometimes winning Scrabble™ is not about coming up with the longest most difficult words, but those tiny words that fit into small places and overlap with other words. Scrabble™ players will often take the time to memorize the list of two-letter words and three-letter words. It may seem like they know many words, but actually they just know how to spell many words. Many players won't be able to tell you what they mean, but they will be able to tell you that the word is in the official dictionary.

Alternate talk:

(Ask students to define some difficult words.) Don't worry. Professional Scrabble™ players probably can't tell you what most of those words mean either. But they know how to spell them and they know that they exist in the English language.

---

Feldman, David. 2004. *Do Elephants Jump?* New York: HarperCollins. Grades 7–12

Do I have a volunteer who will recite the days of the week for me? Do you all think he (or she) said "Monday" or "Mondee?" It turns out that most dictionaries offer both pronunciations, and actually many people in the world say Tuesdee rather than Tuesday. If you were ever curious about odd occurrences in life such as why there are black specks on corn chips and why orange juice tastes bad after you brush your teeth and why staples stick together, you can consult one of David Feldman's many books of unique questions and answers. You can even use the address and e-mail address in the back of the book to submit your own questions; they might be answered in the next book.

Alternate talk:

What is a bizarre question that you don't know the answer to, such as why is a firefighter's hat shaped the way it is? Or why do we put sprinkles on ice cream? (They will most likely ask a question that is not in the book.) Well, that's not in this book, but you can get many answers to many fascinating questions in *Do Elephants Jump?*

Fields, Terri. 2002. *After the Death of Anna Gonzales*. New York: Henry Holt.
Grades 7–12

(Read parts of, or all of, a poem from the book. Try Lynn Helter's.)

> "Why did Anna have to kill herself now?
> I don't mean to be rude or anything,
> But
> She certainly didn't have any consideration.
> Everyone knows how important the pep assembly is going to be . . .
> I tried to cut the ROTC flag raising,
> But that didn't fly with the principal . . . (pp. 52–53).

Anna Gonzales has killed herself, and, in this book, many of the people from the school give their opinions. Lynn is upset that she won't get to show off her cheerleading after all her hard work organizing the pep assembly because it will be cancelled. One guy uses it as a way to get out of practice and another just screams.

---

Flake, Sharon G. 2003. *Begging for Change*. New York: Hyperion.
Grades 6–9

Name something you want more than anything else. (Wait for responses.) For Raspberry Hill in *Begging for Change* by Sharon Flake, all she wants is money. She wants it so badly that she even steals from her friend and neighbor to get it. This is a continuation of her story in *Money Hungry*.

---

Flake, Sharon. 2004. *Who Am I without Him? Short Stories about Girls and the Boys in their Lives*. New York: Hyperion.
Grades 8–12

Girls can sometimes get a little crazy when it comes to boys. Britney Spears stole the father of a woman's child before the baby was even born. (Use current examples of celebrities fighting over or stealing each other's boyfriends or husbands.) *Who Am I without Him?* is a collection of short stories about girls who really love their guys. One girl stays with her boyfriend even though she sees him with other women because she doesn't think she is pretty enough to get anyone else. Another girl has these bumps all over her face yet she dreams of the perfect boy asking her out. And another girl writes a letter to a magazine about the boy she wants to steal from her friend only to get a surprising answer. So these are just some of the stories about girls who have trouble with boys and the trouble they cause them.

---

Fleischman, Paul. 1995. *A Fate Totally Worse Than Death*. Cambridge, MA: Candlewick.
Grades 7–12

" . . . Think of someone who is so popular and perfect that sometimes you just wish something bad would happen to them. In *A Fate Totally Worse Than Death*, the students get their wish. Something starts happening to the popular crowd. They start aging. They get wrinkles. Their hair falls out. They can hardly walk. Now they have to find out who is behind this" (Bromann, 1999:63).

Alternate talk:

(Mention popular series that teens may have read in the past or that are available now that this book may be parodying.)

---

Fleischman, Paul. 1997. *Seedfolks*. New York: HarperTrophy.
Grades 4–9

(If you like to use props, consider having a planter with dirt inside and give the students seeds. Have them take turns putting the seeds in the pot. Then either you or a student can place the pot by the window.) In *Seedfolks*, a variety of people, even the unlikely ones, start a garden to brighten up the neighborhood. It's really short. And thanks for helping us brighten up the library (or whatever room you are in).

---

Fleischman, Paul. 1998. *Whirligig*. New York: Holt.
Grades 7–12

Let's say you're at a party. Only when you get there you realize that you are the only one wearing a brightly colored shirt. No one bothered to tell you that you were supposed to wear either black or white to be part of the different pieces in a human chess game. So as if that were not embarrassing enough, up comes this girl you really like. You think she's going to start hitting on you but, instead, she calls you a leech and tells you to stop following her around. You are humiliated and decide you have to get out of that party. You've been drinking. I know no one in this room would do anything like that, but for the story let's say that's what happens. You get in your car, you take off, and you decide you just can't take it anymore. You start thinking about what happened at the party and everything that is going on in your life and you just can't do it anymore. You close your eyes, let go of the steering wheel, and get ready to die. (Close your eyes, lift your arms in the air and open your eyes.) When you open your eyes you find that you didn't succeed in killing yourself, but you did succeed in killing someone else. And the mother of this girl has asked that your punishment not be to serve time, pay a fine, or do community service. No. Instead, you are asked to make these whirligigs. And if you don't know what they are they are those lawn ornaments that spin around on the top. And you are asked to make four of these that look like, or in some way represent, the girl you killed. You are then given a bus ticket to travel to the four corners of the United States to place one of these whirligigs in each corner to remind yourself of what you have done. That is what happens in the book *Whirligig* by Paul Fleischman. (Adapted from Bromann, 1999:62).

Freyburger, Nancy. 2003. *Gogh Is Gone*. Bloomington, IN: 1st Books Library.
Grades 10–12

You might not like it when your parents harp on you to do your homework. Or they really want you to go to a specific college or go into a certain profession. Well, that's not the case in one of the short stories in *Gogh Is Gone*. In this story, the girl's parents threaten to send her to a school for performing arts if she doesn't stop doing so much math and if she doesn't stop being so organized. It is not until a disastrous event occurs that her parents soon change their minds. The author is a delightful woman who has many stories to tell and this is just one of them. Writing is one of many careers she has had. One of her latest was as a hotel nanny and she is writing a book about these experiences as well. The first part of the book is a short novella and the rest are short stories, so there is probably one in it that will relate to you.

Frost, Helen. 2003. *Keesha's House*. New York: Farrar, Straus & Giroux. Grades 7–12

There are probably times when you have trouble at home or with your friends or your girlfriend or boyfriend or at school and you just wish you could get away. In one town, the kids have a place to go. It's Keesha's house. Here you may find boys who have been kicked out of the house, a pregnant teenager, and a girl who can't stand the abuse from her stepfather. It is a place run by Joe. He was saved years ago by a woman in that very house. When she died, she left him the house, and so now he just takes in young people who need a place to stay with no questions asked. Some come and go. Some come for a short time. And some might be there forever.

Frost, Helen. 2004. *Spinning through the Universe*. 2004. New York: Farrar, Straus & Giroux. Grades 4–6

Can someone tell me something interesting that happened to you at home or at school recently? Are you failing a class because you have to work late? Did you get in a fight with a friend? Fall down the stairs? Anything? (Allow one student to tell you the story). Okay. Now let's put that into a poem. To make it simple, let's do a haiku. The first line needs to be 5 syllables, the second 7, and the last 5. (Give an example of a five-syllable first line from the student's story. Then ask the students to create the next two lines. Instead, you could ask each student to write a haiku about his or her day, giving an example from your day and then asking some of them to share their poems.) The book *Spinning through the Universe* is a collection of poems from students in one class. Some write about their parents who are sick or who have died. Some write about their crushes or their lack of interest in boys. And some talk about their pets or their belongings, like a stolen bike. They are all different, just like all of your stories are different. At the end of the book it explains the types of poems used to tell the stories and how you can write your own.

Gaiman, Neil. 2002. *Coraline.* New York: HarperCollins.
Grades 5–9

There have probably been times when you were upset with your parents and wished they were more like your friends' parents or the people on TV. In the book *Coraline*, Coraline is bored. Her parents are too busy to make good meals for her or to play with her or entertain her. They just keep working and expect her to find things to do on her own. One day she discovers a door in her kitchen. Her mom tells her that it is nothing, but it opens, and when she walks inside the apartment looks just like her own. Soon she sees her parents, only they aren't really her parents. They just look like her parents, but these parents want to play with her and cook her meals. When she goes back home she finds out that her parents have disappeared. She has to decide if she should try to find out what happened to her own parents or stay with these new parents, who might not be as great as they seem.

Gardner, Graham. 2004. *Inventing Elliot.* New York: Dial Books
Grades 7–10

A boy is beaten up at school just because he is a nerd. He doesn't have the right clothes. He can't play sports. He looks scared. Finally he is so badly beaten that he switches to a new school. Here he does not want to be noticed. He doesn't want to stand out. He has to say the right things. So when the popular boys start talking to him he has to be tough. He thinks they will finally leave him alone. Only this time they want him on their side. He did such a good job at pretending to be cool that they want him to join their gang, the Guardians. So now it is Elliot's turn, in *Inventing Elliot*, to choose someone to be the abuser, someone to be abused, and the punishment. He has to decide if he should make someone suffer as much as he did and if he could actually make changes by taking people he likes off the hit list, or if there would be consequences if he doesn't follow the rules.

Getz, Peter. 1996. *Frozen Man.* New York: Henry Holt.
Grades 4–9

On an episode of the television show *Saturday Night Live*, there was once a joke about a man who was hiking and found an ancient man buried in the snow and ice. The joke was that we would then find the hiker in another 100 years or so. *Frozen Man* is the story of finding and identifying a man who was about 5,000 years old. This was just in 1991. The book goes through the process of how the body was discovered and how scientists were able to discover the age of the man, his occupation, and what happened to him all by the clues in his body, clothing, and position. (Show the pictures from the book. You might want to start with news clippings of recent discoveries.)

Giles, Gail. 2003. *Dead Girls Don't Write Letters*. Brookfield, CT: Roaring Brook Press.
Grades 6–10

Maybe you saw the reality television show *Big Brother*. The show takes about 13 people and puts them in a house together. In each episode they have to vote someone off the show until only one remains and wins. In *Big Brother 5* they had a twist. They had a set of twins who switched places and no one could tell. In the book *Dead Girls Don't Write Letters*, a family gets a letter from their daughter and sister, who was supposed to have died in a fire. She comes back home, but she is not the daughter or sister. (Substitute this example with more current examples of twins or look-alikes, such as celebrities.)

Glancy, Diane. 2002. *Stone Heart: A Novel of Sacajawea*. Woodstock, NY: Overlook.
Grades 10–12

Do you remember anything about Sacajawea? What do you know about her? Well, she was not exactly the guide people make her out to be. In fact, she is hardly mentioned at all in the Lewis and Clark journals. She was actually granted permission to travel on the expedition as kind of a sightseer. The author of *Stone Heart* takes excerpts from the Lewis and Clark journals and invents the story of Sacajawea's going along with them.

Glenn, Mel. 1996. *Who Killed Mr. Chippendale? A Mystery in Poems*. New York: Dutton.
Grades 7–12

You probably listen to your school announcements every day. You probably hear what clubs are meeting and what is for lunch. But one day at

Tower High the message coming from the loudspeaker says, "At approximately 7:30 this morning, the body of one of our teachers was found on the school track . . . . He will be sorely missed (p.8)." The book *Who Killed Mr. Chippendale?* begins when a teacher, Mr. Chippendale, goes running on the track before school and someone in a red, hooded sweatshirt decides to shoot and kill him. This book is written in poems that show the various points of view of the students and teachers in the school. Some students hated Mr. Chippendale for giving them bad grades or catching them cheating, while other students loved him for helping them get into college and encouraging them to do something with their lives. But one of these people is the killer. You have to read the poems and try to figure out for yourself who shot Mr. Chippendale. Since it is written in poetry form, it will only take you about an hour to read.

Alternate talk:

(Read the police captain's possible motives on page 13. "He dissed me." "I needed the money." "He looked at me funny." "I caught him with my. . . ." "He stole from me." "I heard voices." "I tell you it was an accident." "I swear it wasn't personal." "For kicks, man." These were all possible motives a police captain thought of for why someone might have killed a teacher at Tower High School.

---

Going, K. L. 2003. *Fat Kid Rules the World*. New York: G. P. Putnam's Sons.
Grades 7–12

There was this guy Troy, who weighed about 300 pounds. No one liked him at school. He had no friends. Then one day, when he was about to kill himself, he met a musician named Curt. Curt was well liked because he was in a popular band. When Curt meets Troy he gets Troy to pay for some meals. Troy also lets Curt clean up at his house because Curt hates to go home. Troy mistakenly admits he had played drums in the past, and now finds himself the drummer in Curt's band. The thought of this makes him sick, but he is suddenly finding that people pay attention to him since he is Curt's friend and in a band. The author's favorite band is Nirvana and that is how she created the character of Curt MacRae, who is based on Kurt Cobain.

---

Goldstein, Bobbye S. 2003. *Mother Goose on the Loose*. New York: Harry
   N. Abrams.
Grades 6–12

Name a Mother Goose or nursery rhyme. (Have the pages in the book
marked for each nursery rhyme. Locate the one given to you by a student. Give them hints if they can't think of any. Hold up the cartoon,
describe it, and read the caption.) The editor of this book found all the
cartoons in past issues of *The New Yorker* magazine that had to do with
nursery rhymes or fairy tales and compiled them in this book. So if you
are interested in what really happened to the characters from the rhymes,
you can take a look at this.

Alternate talk:

(Give the students cartoons from a newspaper and ask them to come
up with a caption that has to do with a fairy tale or nursery rhyme to fit
the cartoons. They can pretend the cartoon characters are characters
from the tales and rhymes.)

---

Goobie, Beth. 2002. *Sticks and Stones*. Victoria, B.C: Orca Book.
Grades 8–12

(Show the front cover.) Have you ever seen any kind of graffiti or writing on someone's locker or on a bathroom stall? (Follow with a similar
story.) In college I was using the restroom in the library, and I saw comments written on the wall in a stall about how people needed to flush.
Being the environmentalist I was at the time, yet doing a very bad thing,
I wrote after it a phrase I had read in my high school biology book: "If
it's yellow, let it mellow. If it's brown, flush it down." I had completely
forgotten about this, but weeks later I ended up in the same stall and
was shocked to see about five other comments. One said how disgusting I was and another said how I was just trying to make a point about
water conservation. Either way, words have an effect on people. In *Sticks
and Stones* by Beth Goobie, a girl has been labeled a slut because a boy
she went out with is telling lies about her and she has to prove the truth
of the saying that "Names will never hurt you."

---

Greenberg, Gary. 1999. *The Pop-up Book of Phobias*. New York: William Morrow.
Grades 9–12

Are any of you afraid of anything? Do you have any phobias? I am afraid of heights and ghosts. (Name your own fears.) How about you? *The Pop-up Book of Phobias* makes you face your fears by having them pop up right at you. So if you have mysophobia, which is a fear of unsanitary things, a filthy toilet might pop up at you. If you have glossophobia, or the fear of speaking in public places, a microphone will pop up ready for you to talk. (Show the pop-ups.) So face your fears and don't be too afraid of spiders. (Show the spider.)

Alternate talk:

What is aerophobia? (Wait for responses.) The fear of air travel. Ophidiophobia? The fear of snakes. (Continue with other phobias from the book.) These are some of the phobias mentioned in *The Pop-up Book of Phobias*.

Greenberg, Jan. 2001. *Heart to Heart*. New York: Harry N. Abrams.
Grades 6–12

(Show one of the paintings from the book or hold up a different painting or picture of a painting.) Look at this painting and tell me what you think of it. What words come to mind? (Write these down on a board if possible.) You could have been one of the writers of this book. *Heart to Heart* is a collection of poems by well-known authors. They have been asked to write a poem to go along with a selected painting or photograph. They might write about what the characters or objects think or feel or about their own reactions to the picture and their own lives. You might find one of your favorite authors in here or you might try writing your own poems to match the pictures.

Grimes, Nikki. *Bronx Masquerade*. 2002. New York: Dial Books.
Grades 7–12

(Bring two or more students to the front of the room. Ask the class for a topic for a poem. Have each of the selected students create a line of the poem, especially in rap or with a rhythm.) This is one of the ways students write poetry at their school in *Bronx Masquerade*. Every Friday they have a poetry open mike in their class. Students who have never written poetry before start sharing things about their personal lives that no one knew. One girl was hit by her boyfriend. Her poem reads, "I bruise easily" (p. 15). Another girl was talking with someone in the bathroom until she noticed her friend was in the stall, and suddenly she pretended to no longer like that girl. This girl wrote, "You don't want to be me, so you curse and smash the mirror, which gets you what?" (p. 72). A guy was afraid to read a poem because he had dyslexia, but one day he stood up there and read, "Neurological distinction notwithstanding, something in me whispers Freak every time I wriggle out of reading aloud, or have to ask a stranger 'Excuse me, but what does that sign say?' Read me any way you choose. Only please stop asking 'What's his problem?'" (p. 127).

---

Grisham, John. 2003. *Bleachers*. New York: Doubleday.
Grades 8–12

Sports are pretty big at this school, right? Do you fill up the stands on game days? In a town called Messina, 8,000 people manage to fill 10,000 seats every Friday night. Football is the life of the town. Some players leave to play at colleges. Some never leave the town. And some come back. Now the stadium will be filled again, but this time it is because of their coach's death. After 34 years of coaching, he was fired after an accident during a practice. Now that he is dead, all the secrets of the past come out for the Messina Spartans. (You might use the same introduction for the book *Friday Night Lights* by Bissinger.)

---

Haddix, Margaret Peterson. 2004. *The House on the Gulf*. New York: Scholastic.
Grades 5–9

Let's say someone in your family comes home one day and says he or she found this great summer job. The family would house-sit for a couple who moves to New York over the summer, and they could live there for free and get a little extra money. Only when the family moves in there are strange conditions. You can't touch the thermostat even though it is 90 degrees outside. You can't eat off their dishes. You have to lock all their belongings away. The only door that is locked is a closet in the brother's room. You can't tell the neighbors anything about yourselves.

In fact, you shouldn't even be talking to the neighbors. Would you think this was a strange arrangement? Well, in the *House on the Gulf* this is exactly what happens. The brother was cutting the lawn of this couple and now he says he has the job of house-sitting, only something seems a little bit off with this arrangement and his sister tries to figure out what it is.

---

Haddix, Margaret Peterson. 1995. *Running Out of Time*. New York: Aladdin.
Grades 4–9

How many of you have seen the movie *The Village*? Did you like it? Did you guess the ending? Well, you might have guessed the ending more quickly if you had read the book *Running Out of Time* by Margaret Peterson Haddix. The author was considering legal action because the plot of the movie closely resembles the plot of her book (Susman, 2004). You'll have to decide for yourself if she has grounds to sue. In case you have not seen the book or the movie, I won't reveal what happens. But I will tell you that both the movie and the book involve a young girl leaving her village for a place she has never been before in order to get medicine that the town is lacking. When she gets to the new place there is a surprise for her—or maybe more for the reader or audience.

---

Haddon, Mark. *The Curious Incident of the Dog in the Night-Time*. 2004. New York: Vintage.
Grades 7–12

There was once a story on the Oprah show about a boy who was being mauled by pit bulls. A woman saw this, jumped out of her car, and threw herself on the boy so that he would not be killed. Now let's say you saw this happening, do you think you would be able to do the same thing? What if it was a neighbor's dog that you found dead on the lawn? What would you do? In the book *The Curious Incident of the Dog in the Night-Time*, Christopher sees his neighbor's dead dog and is so sad that he goes over to try and comfort and save it. The dog's owner sees this and accuses this autistic boy of murder and sends him to jail. Christopher sets out to find out who was responsible for killing this dog.

---

Hallowell, Janis. 2004. *The Annunciation of Francesca Dunn*. New York: William Morrow.
Grades 8–12

If you could have any super power what would it be? (Wait for answers.) For Francesca Dunn, her power is to heal people. One day a homeless man sees a vision of a woman glowing on the lake. The next day he sees that it is the same woman who serves him his food at the shelter. He vows to protect her, but when he tells others, they want her to heal them. Soon she has people gathering outside her home believing that she is the new Virgin Mary. She soon starts to believe it herself. You have to decide if she really does have any power or if it is all in her head and the heads of everyone else around her.

Hansen, Drew, D. *The Dream: Martin Luther King, Jr. and the Speech That Inspired a Nation*. 2003. New York: Harper Collins.
Grades 9–12

You have probably all heard of the "I have a dream" speech by Martin Luther King, Jr., right? Can anyone recite part of it? Well, did you know that King wasn't even going to use that speech? He had one all prepared but as soon as he saw the reactions of the crowd he abandoned what he was going to say. He had often used the "I have a dream" part of his speech in his sermons. He also used the ending, where he said "let freedom ring" from all different parts of the land, in his speech. Some say he stole parts of it. Some say he took much of it from the Bible. The book *The Dream* first gives you the background about what was going on with the civil rights movement at this time, not only with King but with others. When it gets to the speech, the author places the prepared speech alongside the speech King actually gave along with descriptions of crowd reactions, including those who performed or made speeches. If you have heard the speech before, this book will show you what was happening behind the scenes at that moment. You will feel like you are there. The book may seem long, but the story part only goes to about page 85. If you want to find out more about how the parts of the speech were constructed, you can read on for the analysis.

Hautman, Pete. 2004. *Godless*. New York: Simon & Schuster.
Grades 6–10

There are thousands of religions in the world today. Anyone can start a religion. You have probably heard of the religion Scientology started by the science fiction writer L. Ron Hubbard. I remember the TV commercials that offered his books for free, and sometimes they mail his books to libraries for free to try to gain followers. In the book *Godless*, Jason is forced by his religious parents to attend church and a teen group. He always argues against God and religion in the meetings. So one day he just blurts out that he worships the ten-legged one, and before he knows it he has started a small group of friends praying to the town's water tower. They have their own "bible," and each person has his or her own role. Trouble begins only when they want to fully understand their religion and climb to the top of the tower.

Hesser, Terry Spencer. 1998. *Kissing Doorknobs*. New York: Delacorte Press.
Grades 5–12

Do you know what OCD is? Well, it means obsessive compulsive disorder. For example, if you obsess about cleanliness and wash your hands over and over again. Or you are obsessed with counting and count how many steps it takes you to get to school. You might even have to go back home and start all over again if someone interrupts. Some people live with this problem and are almost unable to function. *Kissing Doorknobs* is based on the author's own experiences with OCD. (Use a similar format for the book *Devil in the Details: Scenes from an Obsessive Girlhood*, by Jennifer Traig.)

Hidier, Tanuja Desai. 2003. *Born Confused*. New York: Push.
Grades 9–12

You have probably heard of those speed-dating services, right? It is where women and men have one to six minutes to talk to each other, and then they move on to the next person. At the end of the night they write down the numbers of the people they liked, and if two people match up the host contacts them. Well, in the book *Born Confused*, Dimple's cousin in India wasn't having much luck with an arranged marriage. The parents had been placing ads but after a family refused her unless she would lighten her skin and get eye surgery so she didn't need glasses, the family resorted to this type of speed-dating service where the women and men would present each other with cards that had stats like family and salary. The guy she chose because she was not wearing her glasses became her husband. But Dimple has her own dating problems in America. She is what she soon finds out is an American Born Confused Desi, or ABCD. She doesn't seem to fit in with the American culture, but since she was born here, she doesn't fit in or understand the Indian culture although everyone expects it of her because her parents were born in India. Her best friend, Gwyn, gets her a date by describing her as the INDIAN girl in school and says the guy is into the Indian thing. The one bit of matchmaking her parents do try is to set her up with the son of their old friend from India with whom they were recently reunited. She thinks badly of him all night and how he is like a mama's boy and is into the same music as her father. But after going with her cousin to an Indian party and seeing that he is the DJ and considered one of the coolest Indians at NYU, she soon changes her mind and finds him one of the most unsuitable suitable partners; only it seems Gwen has beat her to him. Her white friend is so interested in him that she tries to dress like an Indian and participate in all the Indian events, and she wears Dimple's clothing that she herself never wears.

Dimple soon finds out that there is a whole world of ABCDs and she is not alone in her confusion. The only thing she does understand is her camera, which was a gift from her grandfather in India. The pictures are her way of communicating with him even though they don't speak the same language. But because she discovers this new world she begins to ask questions and realizes her parents really are in love and that she enjoys going to the temple with her father and learning about her culture. Although she used to ignore the one other Indian in school because she didn't want to seem like one of them, she now realizes she could date an Indian boy. She even once caught herself referring to herself as a minority, thinking of herself as white in the middle of a party of Indians. (Although the author says she has heard of a situation in which a marriage was arranged in this way, another Indian woman told me that this would not occur.)

Hinton, S. E. 2004. *Hawkes Harbor*. New York: Tom Dohgerty.
Grades 10–12

Some of you may have read or seen the movies for the books *The Out-siders, Tex,* or *Rumble Fish*. The author wrote those over 20 years ago. She hasn't written a novel since, although she has written a few books for children. This is her first book written for adults and it is very different from her others. So, if you like *The Outsiders* you might not like this one. It is more of a mystery/horror story. It starts with a young man in a mental hospital who is severely depressed and he seems to be having nightmares over something. He is being kept at this center by his former employer, and before he is ready to be released the employer comes and takes him back to the town where he came from. You slowly find out details of his past. He used to work on ships and do anything illegal for money. His adventurous side made him so curious about the haunted island with a buried treasure off the coast of Hawkes Harbor that he decides to go there. Only he sees something there that terrifies him and changes his life forever.

Hobbs, Will. 1998. *The Maze*. New York: Morrow Junior Books.
Grades 6–12

If you have ever found yourself in detention, life could be worse. Rick has been in foster care and in court many times. This time he can't say he is sorry to the judge so he is sent to a harsh detention facility for six months. He could have made it through, only he reports that one of the guards accepted money from a maintenance man. Now his social worker has been fired and he is afraid he will be killed, so he decides to escape. He ends up in the canyons with a man who takes him in, only he soon finds that crime is not only on the streets and in prison.

Hoffman, Alice. 2002. *Indigo*. New York: Scholastic.
Grades 5–10

Two boys were found in the ocean. They had webbing between their toes and fingers. They loved to swim, and they only ate fish. Their nicknames were Trout and Eel. (You might ask students to guess about these children.) The boys were adopted, but they never felt quite comfortable in this town, where a dam had been built to control the water. Eventually, a woman enters their home and decides to ask the boys to run away with her to the ocean.

---

Hoffman, Nina Kiriki. 2003. *A Stir of Bones*. New York: Viking.
Grades 6–9

Have any of you ever seen a ghost before? (Tell your ghost sightings or sightings from others. I often tell how I saw a little girl walking up the stairs in my parents' house and two weeks later my house burnt down. I was sure it was a warning.) Everyone likes to pretend that there might be ghosts or something hidden away in an old abandoned house. Kids sneak into cemeteries to find Bloody Mary and dare each other to go into abandoned places. In *A Stir of Bones*, a rich girl overhears her housekeeper's son and his friends talking about sneaking into a nearby house. Susan never has any fun and she doesn't have many friends, so she asked if she could be invited along. So they make plans to go to this old haunted house and they find just what they are looking for. The house shakes and dust flies all over and sounds come from different places. They think the boy in the house is doing a really good job of making the house seem haunted until they find out that he is really dead.

---

Holden, Greg. 2001. *Literary Chicago: A Book Lover's Tour of the Windy City*. Chicago: Lake Claremont Press.

(Find a similar book about a city near you.) If you have ever been to Chicago, you have probably walked by places like Union Station or the Museum of Science and Industry, but you probably never thought about the books that may have taken place in these locations. *Literary Chicago* tells you about such places as well as statues of literary figures and places where you can buy a variety of books. So, if you like books, you might want to take a look at this before your next trip to Chicago.

---

Jackson, Donna M., and Charlie Fellenbaum. 1996. *The Bone Detectives: How Forensic Anthropologists Solve Crimes and Uncover Mysteries of the Dead*. Boston: Little, Brown.
Grades 4–10

(Have an ink pad and a pad of paper.) There has been a crime at this school, and I need to fingerprint some people to see if they match the fingerprints at the scene of the crime. (Have some enlarged fingerprints already available on the wall.) You are all off the hook. None of your fingerprints match. But fingerprinting is just one of the ways that forensic scientists can help solve crimes. *Bone Detectives* is the story of a case in which a skeleton was discovered in 1987 at a Boy Scout camp in Missouri. In this book you can find out how detectives and medical examiners and scientists can find out about a person's physical appearance and even some things about their lives based on just a skeleton that is years old. In one such project, they were able to reconstruct the skull and see what this woman might have looked like. They found a picture of a woman missing around that time that matches it almost exactly. (Show the picture.) So take a look at this book if you want to see how science can help solve crimes. You might also try David Owen's *Hidden Secrets*.

---

Jacobs, Thomas A. 2003. *They Broke the Law—You Be the Judge: True Cases of Teen Crime*. Minneapolis: Free Spirit.
Grades 8–12

If you have ever seen *Judge Judy, People's Court, Boston Legal* or any other court or law program on TV, you have heard judges make decisions on the evidence and testimonies provided. Now you can be the judge in the book *They Broke the Law—You Be the Judge: True Cases of Teen Crime*. There are 21 different cases. You get the background of the accused, the facts of the case, and some personal letters from the defendants. After you decide, the book gives you the facts of what actually occurred and what the person is doing now. So in the case of Breanne, she broke into a car, stole the car and a credit card, and bought car parts with the credit card, forging her name. She had been in the courts multiple times over the years, so even after she wrote a letter to the judge she ended up in an adult court. Now she has a job and a child. You can decide if the judge made the right decision.

---

Jimenez, Francisco. 1997. *The Circuit: Stories from the Life of a Migrant Child*. Boston: Houghton Mifflin.
Grades 4–12

What have been some of the best Christmas gifts you have ever received? You are pretty lucky because Panchito and his family don't get much of anything on Christmas. They left Mexico to become migrant workers in

California. They often lived in one-room shacks with just enough money to pay for their daily expenses. One Christmas, the family only had enough money for a few pieces of candy as their Christmas gifts. This was hard on Panchito and his brothers and sister because he sometimes went to school with people who had more than him. The story starts when he is younger, moves on to how he helps his family pick strawberries from the fields, and then to his high school years when he and his brother are old enough to go to dances. I don't normally tell the ends of books, but in the end the police come to his school to take him away, and you don't find out what happens until the second book, *Breaking Through*.

Johnson, Angela. 2003. *A Cool Moonlight*. New York: Dial.
Grades 4–8

What if someone told you that you had to stay inside all day and couldn't go out? You couldn't go to school with your friends. You could only go out at night when everyone was doing homework and sleeping. Would you like that? In *Cool Moonlight*, Lila can't go outside. If she does she has to be covered up or have sunscreen all over her all the time. She has a disease that causes the sun to burn her skin almost immediately. Her vacations have to be at night. Her shopping is done at night. Her drives through town all have to happen at night.

Johnson, Angela. 2003. *The First Part Last*. New York: Simon & Schuster.
Grades 7–12

There is a 16-year-old boy who suddenly finds out that he has become a father and he has to be the one to take care of the child. The book is called *The First Part Last* because it is written backwards, starting with the boy taking care of his child. You don't find out what happened to the mother until the end. The chapters alternate between the past and present. The book is also pretty short and skinny, so it won't take long to read. If you want to know what happens to the boy's daughter you can read *Heaven*. It was written before *The First Part Last*, but it is about Bobby's child.

Johnson, Angela. 1998. *Gone from Home: Short Takes*. New York: Dell Laurel-Leaf.
Grades 9–12

Has anyone had any bad luck recently? Fallen? Didn't do well on a test? Lost something? Anyone? (Gather three or more stories. Now put them together. So if someone said she fell down the stairs, another said she failed a test, and another said she lost something, your story might go like this: "One day a student fell down the stairs on the way to take a test. When she got to class she realized she had lost the paper she took notes on, which they were allowed to have during the test. Because she didn't study, she failed. What bad luck." In the book *Gone from Home*, there are short stories about many things. One is about a girl who had really bad luck. (You could read the story since it is only a page long, or summarize it). A girl was walking with her mom when she knocked into a flower guy and he lost all the flowers. The mom yelled and the flower man wanted money for the flowers. The girl ran away and a bucket fell off a ladder and hit her on the head, landing her in a hospital where the flower guy had delivered flowers. In another story, a girl is walking down the street and sees a man carrying a bunch of empty egg cartons. She asks the man why he carries these egg cartons with him. The man tells her that he lost the will to live and so he was standing on the tracks waiting to die. But just one hundred yards away, the train derailed and all these egg cartons flew all over the side of the road, so the man picked them up and carries them with him as a reminder of how strange and dumb life can be.

Jones, Patrick. 2004. *Things Change*. New York: Walker.
Grades 8–12

Everyone has trouble asking out someone he or she likes. In the book *Things Change*, Johanna decides to make the first move. She asks a guy for a ride home. He is kind of a bad boy and she is kind of a good girl, but she decides to go for it. In the car she asks him to kiss her. He freaks out but soon decides to take her up on her offer. Only maybe she shouldn't have. She loses her best friend when her new guy tells the friend that Johanna is a lesbian, and she finds out that her new boyfriend might be more of a bad boy than she had thought.

Alternate talk:

In *Things Change* a girl gets brave and asks a guy to kiss her. They actually become boyfriend and girlfriend. She thinks everything is great, until he starts to hit her.

---

*Jump: Poetry and Prose by Writerscorps Youth.* 2001. San Francisco: WritersCorps Books.
Grades 4–12

What do you think about when you hear the word pizza? (Wait for answers). Is there a food that you can't eat because it makes you think about something bad, or maybe you puked after you ate it? *Jump* is a book of poetry written by students your age. One of the poems is called "Pizza."

> I loved pizza from the first time I ate it. I don't even remember when I took the first bite.

> But at the age of 8, I noticed that my family was eating pizza every day. Mom was working and Dad was like a housewife. When it was dinner time, he would leave his four kids with money to order pizza. I loved pizza, but eating it almost every day was making me sick.

> Everything changed in my family after eating pizza more than 30 times a month. One day we found out that Dad was cheating on Mom. Knowing why he always left us with money to order pizza made me sick. It was three years later when I finally had the stomach to eat pizza again (p. 117, Dolly Sithonnolat, 17, Ida B. Wells High School).

This is just one of the poems about family, friendship, and life that are in the book *Jump*. The students belong to a writer's workshop in San Francisco. They have teachers help them learn to write, and then every year they publish a book of their writing.

---

Keizer, Garret. 2002. *God of Beer.* New York: HarperTempest.
Grades 8–12

I know you have never been to a party where people were drinking, but at Willoughby Union High School they do have these parties. One day in class, one of the teachers asks the students what was most important to people in their town, and one student answered, "Beer." This led to a class protest project, even though it was not approved by the teacher, and a group of students decided to set up a party where people would not know if they were drinking beer or not. But then the police came.

Alternate talk:

What is the most important thing to people in this school or town? Well, for the people in the book *God of Beer* it is beer.

---

Klebanoff, Susan. 1999. *Ups & Downs: How to Beat the Blues and Teen Depression*. New York: Price Stern Sloan.
Grades 7–12

Name some things you like to do that make you happy. People often forget what makes them happy when they feel depressed. Ever notice when people are sad they play sad songs? Shouldn't people play upbeat music when they are sad? Remembering what makes you happy is just one of the ways to beat depression that are mentioned in this book.

Alternate talk:

(Give the quiz on mental attitude on page 51. Read some questions of the signs of depression on page 38. Read the list of triggers for students to identify what might set them off on page 20.)

---

Klise, Kate. 1999. *Letters from Camp*. New York: Avon Books.
Grades 4–8

How many of you have ever gone away to summer camp before, even if just for a week? Girl Scout or Boy Scout camp? Camping with your family? (Depending on how many answer yes, continue with the following questions.) How many of you had fun at camp? How many of you didn't? Well, just be lucky you did not go to Camp Happy Harmony. *Letters from Camp* is about a camp that was started by an old folk band called the Harmonys. Although the letters home said it was started so that siblings could start to live together in harmony, the kids soon find out something different. Through the letters they write home, but that never make it home, they tell of how they get no food to eat and how their belongings are taken from them. They can only listen to music by the Harmonys and have to wear prom dresses. They take classes like "Fishing for Compliments" and "The Art of Vacuuming." The book even shows you their budget, where most of the money goes to food for the director and staff. Something is wrong and the kids at the camp have to expose the truth. How many of you would like to sign up for Camp Happy Harmony?

---

Koon, Jeff, and Andy Powell. 2003. *Wearing of This Garment Does Not Enable You to Fly: 101 Real Dumb Warning Labels*. New York: Free Press.
Grades 8–12

You may have heard the urban legend about the man who set his cruise control in his Winnebago on 70 mph and then got up to walk around, and, of course, the vehicle crashed. The story goes that he was awarded a couple million dollars because there was no warning in the manual. You might remember when a woman spilled hot coffee on herself at McDonald's and won about $3 million because of it. Since then, more companies have put warning labels on their products. Jeff Koon and Andy Powell, who started dot com careers, put together the book *Wearing of This Garment Does Not Enable You to Fly: 101 Real Dumb Warning Labels* with many of the most obvious warnings out there. For instance, McDonald's now has the label "Caution: Hot" on their coffee cups. A package of Hormel pepperoni reads, "Do not eat packet." The warning on the Bowl Fresh Toilet Cleaner reads, "Safe to use around pets and children, although it is not recommended that either be permitted to drink from the toilet." And Mr. Bubbles Bath Bubbles reads "not for human consumption." This book has many more warning labels for things that you won't believe people might actually try. (Select from a variety of dumb warning labels.)

---

Koontz, Dean. 2004. *Life Expectancy*. New York: Bantam.
Grades 9–12

(Use the fortune-telling opening I suggest for other books.) I've been reading a bunch of books on fortune-telling lately, and I wanted to see if any of you would let me practice on you. I'm not very good yet. (Select a student or two. Hold a student's hand and start making predictions about things they will do or funny things about their relationships.) I see a girl. I'm not sure if she is a friend or more, but she has brown hair and is wearing a sweater. She is kind of short. I also see something really good happening to you on March 5, 2020. Remember that date. (Only do this to one or two students, as many will want to have their fortunes told. When they ask for their fortunes told outside of class, make sure to tell them you only do it in class.) Well, I am not very good at this, but I wouldn't have to be if I were Jimmy's grandfather in the book *Life Expectancy* by Dean Koontz. On the night that Jimmy was about to be born, his grandfather, Josef, who had suffered from a stroke and who was thought to be able to utter no words started to spew out predictions about Jimmy's birth and life. The first was that he would be 20 inches long, eight pounds ten ounces, he would be born at 10:46 p.m., and he would have a condition called syndactyly, meaning his toes would be fused together. Jimmy's father, Rudy, thought it was amazing that his father could pronounce such a word after having a stroke. Josef then started to name dates in the future that would result in terrible situations for his grandson and warned him not to trust the clown. Jimmy's father wrote these dates on the back of a free circus ticket he was given. The doctors thought Josef made a complete recovery, but at exactly 10:46 p.m., he died at the same moment Jimmy was born. On the way to visit his wife and new son, Rudy came across the clown. The clown had just shot the doctor who had delivered his (the clown's) baby but allowed the wife to die. Years later, on September 14, 1994, when Jimmy would be 20, it was time for the first terrible day to occur. He knew he couldn't avoid it and that no matter what he did fate would follow him. So, as planned, he walked into the town library where he witnessed the librarian being shot and he was taken hostage along with another woman. This was only the beginning of the terrible things yet to come. But he knew that if there were more days, he would at least survive the days for now, even if he were to lose a limb or be paralyzed.

---

Korman, Gordon. 2003. *Jake Reinvented*. New York: Hyperion.
Grades 7–12

Have you ever seen the shows *Extreme Makeovers* or *What Not to Wear*? Or the makeovers on *Oprah* or in a teen magazine? In *Jake, Reinvented*, Jake has been reinvented from the nerd he was at his last school. He is having the best parties at school and no one knows where he gets the money for them, although he seems to have a connection with the college kids. He is on the football team, but the only position he can play is the long snapper. And he seems to be stealing away the girlfriend of

one of the guys on his team. But his secrets might end up getting him
in trouble.

---

Korman, Gordon. 2002. *Son of the Mob*. New York: Hyperion.
Grades 7–12

Let's say you are going on a date and you want everything to be perfect.
You ask your brother for advice, you pick out the right clothes, and you
make sure your car is equipped with everything you'll need for a picnic
at a teenage lookout point. Only when it gets to be time to set up for
the picnic, you open the trunk of the car to get the blanket and see that
it is wrapped around a bloody, moving body. This is just what happens
to Alex in *Son of the Mob* by Gordon Korman. Alex's dad and brother
are in the mob. He wants no part of it, but he can't escape it. When he
was a kid, he would go to camp and find his Cracker Jack box was filled
with diamonds. In high school he tried to play football, but quit because
it looked suspicious that he always scored because no one would tackle
him for fear that his mob family would come after them. And, to top it
all off, he also happens to be in love with an FBI agent's daughter.

---

Lahaye, Tim, and Jerry B. Jenkins. 2001. *Left Behind: A Graphic Novel
of the Earth's Last Days*, Book 1, vol. 3. Wheaton, IL: Tyndale House.
Grades 7–12

(Hold up one of the Left Behind novels.) There are over ten books in
this series, and each book is about 400–500 pages long. The story begins when people just start disappearing. They might be sleeping or driving a bus or on a plane. Millions of people just disappear leaving their
clothes and jewelry and families behind. People soon figure out that it
is the Christians who have been taken to Heaven by God, and the others are left to repent or to be left in chaos. If the original books are too
long for you, there are also two other series, one written especially for
teens and this series of graphic novels. These will take you less than 30
minutes to read.

---

Lee, Marie G. 1993. *If It Hadn't Been for Yoon Jun*. New York: Avon.
Grades 6–9

There is probably someone you didn't like when you were a kid, but your
mom made you hang out with him or her anyway. Don't mention any

names. It was probably the son or daughter of a friend of your mom's or a cousin or a neighbor. That's kind of what happens to Alice in the book *If It Hadn't Been for Yoon Jun*. The father who adopted her wants her to meet a new Korean boy at her school, only she doesn't want to be stereotyped by hanging out with him. Then they get stuck being partners for a class project where they have to talk about their heritage. Alice doesn't know if she can handle it or if she will actually get to like Yoon Jun.

---

Lee, Marie G. 1996. *Necessary Roughness*. New York: HarperCollins. Grades 8–12

Is there a soccer team at this school? A football team? Do you think soccer and football are the same? Would someone who knows how to play one of those games be able to play the other even if he or she had never played it before? Well, in the book *Necessary Roughness*, Chan and his family are new to this Minnesota town. He was a soccer star at his old school in California, but there is no soccer team at his new school so he has to play football instead. This doesn't sit well with the members of his team, especially because he and his sister are the only Asian students at this school.

---

Leman, Kevin. 1998. *The New Birth Order Book: Why You Are the Way You Are*. Grand Rapids, MI: Fleming H. Revell. Grades 9–12

I'm going to name several sets of characteristics and I want you to decide which group of words best describes you. (You could also place these on a PowerPoint® or overhead or present them as a hand out.) The first set is perfectionist, confident, organized, self-centered, not afraid to make decisions, busy, believe you are always right, voracious reader, good problem solver, ambitious, energetic, under control. The second set is social, rebellious, cynical, make friends easily, stubborn, hide opinions, don't admit when you need help, trustworthy, secretive, peacemaker, gets along with others, takes risks. The third set is charming, people oriented, affectionate, attention seeking, relaxed, funny, likable, easy to talk to, don't take no for an answer, manipulative, flaky, talks a lot, gullible, airhead, big ego, spoiled, impatient. If you best fit the first grouping, are you a first born or only child? If you best first the second are you a middle child? If the third, are you a last born child? For how many of you did the words match your own birth order? These are some of the characteristics attributed to each in the book *The New Birth Order*. The book also mentions how marriages between people of the same birth order cause conflict. It tells you about famous presidents and their birth order or other famous people, such as Tom Brokaw.

---

Levine, Gail Carson. 2000. *The Wish*. New York: HarperCollins. Grades 4–8

If you had only one wish, what would it be? Now be very careful. (Wait for responses.) In *The Wish*, by the author of the woman who wrote the book that the movie *Ella Enchanted* was based on, a girl meets a woman on the subway who grants her one wish. She makes the mistake of asking to be the most popular girl at her school. It does work. She is surrounded by friends who endlessly compliment her. However, she will be graduating that school this year and is worried she won't be as popular at her next school.

---

Levithan, David. 2003. *Boy Meets Boy*. New York: Alfred A. Knopf. Ages 8–12

Think back to your first childhood memory. Think back to when you were in kindergarten. What do you remember? (You may choose to take responses). Well, in the book *Boy Meets Boy*, Paul looks through the report cards for kids in his class and he sees that his kindergarten teacher wrote "Paul is definitely gay" on his report card. He looks through the others and notices that no other student received this comment. In third grade he ran for class president with the slogan "Vote for me . . . I'm gay." His opponent ran with "Vote for me . . . .I'm not gay." So since the time he was only a child, Paul had known who he was. That is not the problem. His problem is just like everyone else's. He has trouble with relationships and with his friends.

---

Little, Jason. 2002. *Shutterbug Follies*. New York: Doubleday. Grades 11–12

There is a girl who is working at one of those one-hour photo-developing places. To pass the time she takes a look at the pictures others have developed. There are dogs, birthday parties, weddings, but one roll has some disturbing photos on it. They are pictures of dead bodies in coffins. Then a stranger comes in claiming to be a photojournalist. His pictures are all of bloody murder scenes. Something is not quite right, so Bee sets out to find out if these photos are art or if they are evidence of murders. Since *Shutterbug Follies* is a graphic novel, you can actually see the drawings of the photos.

Alternate talk:

Have you ever wondered if the people behind the counter at the one-hour photo look at your pictures? Well, they probably do. In the graphic novel *Shutterbug Follies* . . .

Lowry, Lois. 2004. *The Messenger*. Boston: Houghton Mifflin. Grades 4–10

How many of you had to read the book *The Giver* or have read it by choice? (I don't tend to ask if students have read other books because they often have not. However, almost all students have had to read *The Giver* and teachers fight over teaching it in their grades.) If you plan on reading it, don't listen because I am going to give away the ending. You might remember that Jonas slides down a hill and we don't know if he survives or not. Although *The Messenger* is not his story, it is another book by Lois Lowry that gives us hope that Jonas did survive. In this story there is a town where people go to escape the cruel rules in their original town. People are given jobs and if they came from a cruel society they learn to give up bad habits such as lying and stealing. Newcomers are welcome. But now one of the townspeople wants to stop letting people enter since they are running out of food and supplies, such as fish, to sustain the community. There is a strange machine called the gaming machine that people use for trading; only when a young boy goes to witness the trading experience he finds that people don't come with anything to trade. Matty has to find out what it is that they are trading if they come empty handed and how this changes people for the worse.

Lupica, Mike. 2004. *Travel Team*. New York: Philomel Books. Grades 5–12

Michael Jordan was cut from the sophomore basketball team in high school and we all know what happened to him. Danny, in the book *Travel Team* by sports writer Mike Lupica, is cut from the seventh-grade basketball team because he is too short, even though he is one of the best players in town. His dad was a basketball star in his youth, but his career was ruined after a car accident. Danny is devastated that he can't play, but he gets his chance to prove himself when his distant father steps up and starts a new seventh-grade travel team in town. There are short players on this team so they have to find them, and eventually a new coach, in unusual places.

---

Maguire, Gregory. 2004. *Leaping Beauty*. New York: HarperCollins. Grades 5–9

You may have seen the movie or read the book *Ella Enchanted*. If you haven't, it is about a girl who is given the gift of obedience by a cruel fairy. This means that she must do whatever anyone says for all her life. The book *Leaping Beauty* has a similar story. It is a collection of fairy tales; only the characters are animals rather than humans so the traditional tales are kind of changed around a little. The first story is like *Ella Enchanted*. A frog gets the cruel gift of death from the Old Hornet. She says, "Before your first birthday . . . you shall bite down on a stray explosive from some stupid human engineering project, and you shall blow yourself to smithereens" (p.7). Obedience sounds a little better. Fortunately, the bishop of the beetles had not yet offered his gift so he gave the gift that this young frog would just cry when she bit down on the explosives.

Alternate talk:

If a fairy were to give you one gift, what would you want that to be?

---

Marchetta, Melina. 2003. *Saving Francesca*. New York: Alfred A. Knopf. Grades 8–12

How would you like it if this school suddenly became a girls' school, and the boys had to go to a different school across town? In the book *Saving Francesca*, Francesca wishes this were still true. Her all-girls parochial school only goes to grade 10, and most of the girls go to a different girls' school. But St. Sebastian's all-boys' school just turned co-ed and Francesca's mother—who won't get out of bed to go to work anymore—wants her to go there. There are only 30 girls at this school and 750 boys. They have some demands, like being able to play sports and participating in the school play, but that takes time along with getting the boys to treat you fairly and maybe even getting a date out of it.

---

Marsden, John. 1997. *Dear Miffy*. Sydney, Australia: Macmillan.
Grades 11–12

You have probably passed a note or sent an e-mail or sent a letter and immediately regretted it. Or maybe you have written a letter and decided it probably wasn't a good idea to send it. In *Dear Miffy*, Tony is somewhere that is not really identified. He keeps writing letters to his old girlfriend, Miffy, only he never sends them. He writes about all the good times they had sneaking away together. She was from a rich family and he was not, so they hated each other until they were in detention together. But suddenly they got closer. He wonders if it is because she used him as a weapon against her mother. But then he became the weapon against her mother. Like many of John Marsden's books, you are slowly given clues as to where Tony is and what he did to get there.

---

Marsden, John. 1991. *Letters from the Inside*. New York: Bantam Doubleday Dell.
Grades 7–12

Has anyone ever had a pen pal before? Does anyone still have a pen pal? (You might add your own pen pal stories). Well, before the Internet was popular, people met pen pals through school assignments or through magazines or newspaper ads. That's what Mandy does in the book *Letters from the Inside*. Only after a while her pen pal stops writing to her, and she has to figure out why.

---

Marsden, John. 1995. *Tomorrow When the War Began*. Boston: Houghton Mifflin.
Grades 8–12

"You know how the kids in the movie *Halloween H20* all go off camping and when they return they find their school has been terrorized by Michael Myers? Well, in *Tomorrow When the War Began*, the kids all go off camping, and when they return to town everyone is gone. They have to find out what happened and what to do about it—while surviving on their own" (Bromann, 1999:63). (If your teens no longer follow older horror films or don't remember this one, use another example of a movie, or tell them that this is what happened in this movie as they will surely have seen or heard of the *Halloween* series.)

---

McBay, Bruce. 2003. *Waiting for Sarah*. Victoria, B.C.: Orca Book.
Grades 6–12

There was this guy who got into an accident. He can't play sports or be in P.E. anymore, so he gets to help out on the school yearbook instead. He spends a lot of time by himself looking through old yearbooks until one day this girl starts to visit him. She comes to him covered in blood and then runs away. He has to help her, but he doesn't know where to find her. He asks in the office and finds out that there is no one by that name at the school. He does some research and finds out that she was murdered years ago. (You might want to leave out the last line and allow students to discover it for themselves.)

---

McDonald, Janet. 2003. *Twists and Turns*. New York: Farrar, Straus & Giroux.
Grades 7–12

How many of you know what you want to do when you graduate high school? For those of you who have no idea, don't worry; Keeba and Teesha have no idea either. One of their friends is going to college. Another is pursuing acting, but they are stuck in the projects with not-so-perfect grades and no money. A woman asks them what their talents are and when they say braiding hair, they get the idea not only to braid hair for cash in their home and in others' homes, but to rent a shop and open their own hair-braiding business. But even though they had a great first day, it is not as easy, fun, or profitable as they had hoped.

---

McFarlane, Evelyn and James Saywell. 2001. *If . . . Questions for Teens*. New York: Villard.
Grades 6–12

"If you had to wear a uniform to school, but you could design it, what would it look like?" (p. 44). "If, in biology, the teacher announced that the class would dissect one student, who would you vote to be used as the subject?" (p. 53). Now this doesn't mean the student will die. It just means you get to see what that person looks like inside. "If you were to pick the song whose lyrics best describe your life right now, what song would it be?" (p. 59). These are just some of the questions you can ask yourself and your friends in *If . . . Questions for Teens*. (Ask more of the questions from the book and listen to some of the answers.)

McGraw, Jay. *Life Strategies for Teens*. 2000. New York: Simon & Schuster.
Grades 7–12

I am going to name different cliques in school and you decide which one you best fit into. Goody-two-shoes, prom queen, tease, jock, drama mama, teacher's pet, gossip, slacker, perfecto, druggies, granola, glamour-puss, braniacs, greasers, pig pens, minions, Marilyn Manson . . . Are there any others I missed? Well, these are also some of the roles that Jay McGraw, son of Dr. Phil from *Oprah* and *The Dr. Phil Show*, says we play. He asks you to think about what role you play and ask yourself if it is getting you the treatment you want. He says that getting stuck in these roles hinders you from possible success. The book also gives other ideas to become successful and have a better life in high school and in your future.

McNamee, Graham. 2003. *Acceleration*. New York: Wendy Lamb Books.
Grades 8–12

Now if you came across a diary or journal that someone left in class or in his or her room, would you read it? In *Acceleration,* Duncan works at the train station in the lost-and-found department. He is allowed to take items left there after several months. He usually takes clothes, but one day he comes across someone's diary. He starts to read it and finds out that it is the diary of a serial killer. He thinks the owner of the diary plans to kill women on the subway so he uses the clues in the diary to try and find the man.

McPhee, Phoebe. 2002. *The Alphabetical Hookup List: A–J*. New York: Pocket Books.
Grades 10–12

Is there a guy in this room or at your school whose name starts with an A? Okay. He'd be first. B? Second. C? Third. Well, if these guys were lucky enough to be one of the guys at Pollard University at the time this book was written, then they would have been one of the first to be kissed by these three roommates: Celeste, Jodi, and Ali. These girls are freshmen at college. They expected to have a single room but because of room shortages ended up in a triple. They are very different, but they still have the same trouble with men. One found her longtime boyfriend who came with her to Pollard University in the bathroom with another girl, another found out her boyfriend likes men, and the third has a long-distance boyfriend. They are tired of their men troubles and decide there are too many men to waste time on just one, so they devise the alphabetical hookup list where they must all find men whose names start with each letter of the alphabet, in order, and kiss them.

Alternate talk:

Is there anything that you alphabetize? A CD collection? Your books? Well, in *The Alphabetical Hookup List*, the girls choose their boyfriends by the alphabetic order of their names.

---

Muharar, Aisha. 2002. *More Than a Label*. Minneapolis, MN: Free Spirit Press
Grades 7–12

I'm going to name some cliques or social groups that you might find at schools, and I'd like you to tell me whom you might find in these groups. Abercrombies? Drama kids? Freaks? Gamers? Goody-goodies? Jocks? Players? Scrubs? Techies? Teen queens? Squares? Greasers? Hippies? Metalheads? Rockers? Punks? Preppies? Grunge? Can you name any others? (Use the older labels to see if students can still identify with them. Tell them what year they are from (pp. 18–19). You could also turn it into a Family Feud or Top 10–type game.) The author of *More Than a Label* wrote this book when she was only 17 years old. She talks about why people are labeled, how it makes them feel, and what they can do about it. Teens are asked questions like "Do you label your peers?" and some of their answers are given. So this book is for anyone who has ever been labeled or wants to stop labeling others.

Alternate Talk:

(Start with one or more of the questions in the book about labeling.)

Myers, Walter Dean. 2004. *Shooter*. New York: Amistad.
Grades 6–12

I am sure you all remember the shootings at Columbine High School.
(As time goes by you will need to say, "You may have heard about . . . "
since many of the students now entering junior high and high school
only vaguely recall the incident occurring. ) You may remember that afterwards everyone was trying to figure out why it happened. People
blamed it on the trench-coat mafia, and all across the United States
schools started banning trench coats. Reporters and police talked to
friends and teachers and family and neighbors, but no one really knows
the real reason since the boys killed themselves. In the book *Shooter*
you get an idea why this boy and his friends shot their guns out the window of their high school, wounding and killing some of their classmates.
The book is told from the point of view of the investigators and the students involved. It also includes the diary of one of the shooters.

Myracle, Lauren. 2004. *TTYL*. New York: Amulet Books.
Grades 7–12

How many of you use instant messenger or chat online? Do you know
what LOL stands for? (Laughing out loud.) How about BTW? (By the
way.) BBS? (Be back soon.) And TTYL? (Talk to you later.) (Replace with
any acronyms or chat slang.) Well, there's actually a book written in instant messages among three girlfriends. They talk about religion, boys
they like, their dates, advice for each other, and their family problems,
all online.

Na, An. 2001. *A Step from Heaven*. Asheville, SC: Front Street.
Grades 7–10

My house was just broken into last night. (Hopefully you will receive
some sympathy from the audience. If not wave your arms like you expect some. Use another lie if you choose.) No. Thanks for the sympathy. I was just teasing. But Young Ju in *A Step from Heaven* by An Na
does lie to her classmates. She tells them that her brother has died in
order to get sympathy from her class because she has recently come to
America from Korea and has had trouble adjusting to this new way of
life. She also lies to her father about who she is hanging out with, and

she lies to her friend and makes her drop her off at a different house so no one will know how she lives.

---

Napoli, Donna Jo. 1998. *Sirena.* New York: Scholastic.
Grades 7–12

"Okay, here's a question for the women in the room. If there's a guy you really like, what do you do to get his attention? (Answers often include dressing sexy, hanging out where he does, or just asking him out). Well, in Sirena, the women sing. Guys, do you think that would work for you? A nice sweet voice? It impressed the guy in the movie *American Pie.* Anyway, the women in this book are mermaids, and in order to become immortal they must "get together" with a mortal man. And since their fins kind of turn off most men, the mermaids have to resort to wrecking ships and singing to attract guys. Maybe you girls should give that a try" (Bromann, 1999:63).

---

Nash, Naomi. 2004. *You Are So Cursed!* New York: Dorchester.
Grades 8–12

(I love to start talks with fortune-telling and tricks, so this would be a great book to use for a trick. However, it would be complicated. Wear an oversized sweatshirt or sweater, and pretend that you are hot and take it off. This may not seem very appropriate in some schools, but of course you will have clothing on underneath. Before class, you will have written the name of a student on your arm in marker. Or, you can try to write it while taking the sweater off, like Vickie does.) Now I think there is a student in this room who is going to get in big trouble and that name will appear on my arm. (To avoid possible trouble or being revealed, you could also ask the teacher ahead of time for the name of a student in your room and have that name on your arm before you take off your shirt and reveal the name. Or you could write a phrase like "You are in trouble.") Now, of course you know that I really wrote your name on my arm before class started. But in the book *You Are So Cursed!* Vickie has a similar trick of her own. She is not very popular at her new school, so to prevent people from hurting her she pretends to be a witch. Even her friends think she is a witch. She has everyone at school believing she puts curses on them. So when kids mess up in sports or get in an accident, if they had had a confrontation with Vickie soon before, they swear she has cursed them. One of her little tricks is that when someone is bothering her or her friend, she pretends to take off her shirt while writing the name of the person who is bothering them in wax on her arm beneath her shirt where no one can see, and then she runs ashes over her arms to reveal the name or other messages she has on her arm. But now she is caught. A guy at school practices a magic act that he performs at a senior center and he knows her trick. But now he needs her to help him improve his act, and he says he can help her with new ideas for hers.

---

Naylor, Phyllis Reynolds. 1998. *Sang Spell*. 1998. Atheneum.
Grades 7–12

"You're out hitchhiking. I know you would never do anything like that; you've seen the movies. But let's say your parents are gone. You're on your way to start a new life with your aunt in Texas, and you're not ready to get on that plane. Only you pick the wrong driver. He beats you up, takes your money, and kicks you out into the road. You end up in a town you can't get out of. No matter how far you walk or swim or paddle, no matter how high you climb or hike, you end up in the same place, just like Josh in *Sang Spell*" (Bromann, 1999:63).

---

Nelson, Peter and Judy, and David Larkin. 2000. *The Treehouse Book*. New York: Universe.
Grades 5–12

How many of you have a treehouse? Did you have one when you were younger? Well, treehouses are not just for playing anymore. Some people actually live in treehouses. There is even a treehouse resort in Oregon where you can stay in a treehouse with running water and electricity. The *Treehouse Book* shows you some examples of the some of the many treehouses people have built for work and play. You could also try *Treehouses: The Art and Craft of Living Out on a Limb*.

---

Niffenegger, Audrey. 2003. *The Time Traveler's Wife*. San Francisco: MacAdam/Cage.
Grades 10–12

Raise your hand if you have ever used the Ouija board before? Did anything strange ever happen? (Share your own stories if you have any. For instance, I had been reading a book on the game before a slumber party in high school. I had told no one that I read the main spirit of the board was Seth. While I was not touching the board, that was one of the names spelled out. I completely freaked out. The next day there was a scratch on the board.) Well, in *The Time Traveler's Wife* something similar happened. At a slumber party, Clare is using the game with friends. She does not even have her hand on it when it starts to spell Henry. They all joke with her about her mysterious boyfriend. She denies it, but it is true. Ever since she was a little girl, a strange man has visited her. He just appeared naked one day in the field near her house, and since then he has come back to visit her many times. She knows he is coming from the future, and someday she will catch up with him so they can be married.

---

Northcut, Wendy. 2003. *The Darwin Awards: Survival of the Fittest*. New York: Dutton.
Grades 9–12

You can probably think of many stupid things that you, your friends, or your family have done. But I guarantee they are not as dumb as the news stories and personal accounts in *The Darwin Awards*. A Darwin Award is given to people who have failed to use common sense to solve a problem, such as getting hit by a car while running across the street to catch a half-full beer can, a man who had his cousin saw off his leg with a chain saw to try to get insurance money, a man who was killed by his own booby-trapped home, a man who was shot by the man he was going to steal a gun from, a guy who thought he was going down a laundry chute but ended up in a garbage crusher, a woman who robbed a bank but ran out of gas, and many more. So make sure you think before you act, or you might end up in a future edition of *The Darwin Awards*.

---

Osa, Nancy. 2003. *Cuba 15*. New York: Delacorte Press.
Grades 7–11

"The story you are about to hear is true. None of the names have been changed because no one is innocent" (p. 123). That is how the beginning of Violet's speech goes for the speech competition in the book *Cuba 15*. She has been put in the original comedy category so she had to try and write a funny speech. She chose a dominoes-playing incident with her family that ended up in a fire and a police visit. This is typical for her crazy Polish and Cuban family. Her grandmother has been making visits from Miami to help Violet plan her *quinceañera*. Now Violet is not into fancy dresses. She is not into dresses at all, but the *quinceañera* calls for a big, frilly, pink dress. The *quinceañera* or *quinceañero* is a party given in some Hispanic cultures when a girl or boy turns 15. It is almost like a wedding, but it celebrates becoming a man or woman. Violet is told there should be 14 boys and 14 girls as attendants to make 15 with her, and that her dress should be pink and there should be a theme. But when she gets the book called *Quinceañero for the Gringo Dummy*, she finds out that the party doesn't have to be as strict as her grandmother wants her to believe. She also finds out from her aunt that she could have had a trip to Spain instead, but she was never given this option.

Alternate talk:

(If you are really brave and theatrical, you can start with the beginning of the speech Violet gives about her family's dominoes-and-fire experience by running and yelling fire. Or start with the written beginning of her speech.) Ask if they have heard of the Dummies series.

Palahniuk, Chuck. 2002. *Lullaby.* New York: Anchor Books. Grades 9–12

Can you name any nursery rhymes or lullabies, like "Rock-a-bye Baby"? (Wait for some answers, provide one of your own, or move on). In *Lullaby*, there are 500 copies of the book *Poems and Rhymes from around the World* floating around. It was one of those books that a guy decides to make money on by combining out-of-print poems and rhymes so he can make money but not have to pay to use them. Well, one of the rhymes came from a *Book of Shadows*, or a witch's book, and I can't tell you what it is because in this book, every time someone reads that poem to someone, that person dies.

Alternate talk:

(You could also begin by asking if anyone has ever seen ghosts and tell some stories you know. You could then mention the real estate agent in the story who sells haunted houses over and over again because no one can stand to live in them more than a few weeks. Then lead to the story of the lullaby and how the real estate agent met the journalist investigating the deaths.)

Palmer, Pat, and Melissa Alberti Froehner. *Teen Esteem: A Self-Directing Manual for Young Adults*. San Luis Obispo, CA: Impact.
Grades 6–12

Who wants to tell me something that happened to you today that made you really angry? (Wait for responses. If none are offered, ask for something that happened earlier in the week or year, or mention some of the things that have been mentioned by students in the past. One suggestion to get rid of anger in the book is to be creative. So, for example, if one of the students says something like his mom made him go to school even though he was sick, give him a creative answer like the following.) Well, maybe your mom was abducted by aliens last night, and they made her lose her sense of feeling in her hand. So she couldn't tell that you had a fever. The book suggests the alien answer as one possibility (p. 45). This is just one of the suggestions that *Teen Esteem* suggests to help you focus on something other than your anger. The book contains information on ways to like yourself, how to say no, how to keep yourself from being manipulated, how to make decisions, and more ways to develop self-esteem.

---

Parish, James Robert. 2001. *The Hollywood Book of Death*. New York: Contemporary Books.
Grades 7–12

You know how they always talk about dead pools on the radio, where you guess what celebrity will die next or by the end of the year? Well, some deaths can be predicted, but others are a complete surprise. *The Hollywood Book of Death* talks about celebrities from far in the past to close to the present who have died by accident, murder, natural cause, suicide, or drugs. You might remember Phil Hartman from *Saturday Night Live*, who was murdered by his wife. Or Sonny Bono of Sonny and Cher, who crashed while skiing. Or the rapper Tupac Shakur, who was shot while he was sitting in a car.

Alternate talk:

We're going to play a short game of "Dead or Alive." I will name a celebrity and you tell me if he or she is dead or alive. Okay. Jennifer Aniston. Sammy Davis Jr. Phil Hartman. (Select popular teen stars and some select celebrities from the book. Repeat ending from the first booktalk.)

---

Pascal, Francine. 2004. *The Ruling Class*. New York: Simon & Schuster.
Grades 8–12

How many of you have read the Sweet Valley High series? (Depending
on the responses, say something like "Maybe you are too young," or "Really? So boys like books about twin sisters and their boy troubles?") Well,
when I was in school, Francine Pascal created the Sweet Valley High
series about twin sisters and their high school life with their friends and
boyfriends. There were over one hundred of them. Even though it was
about high school, we were reading this in seventh and eighth grade.
(Share your own stories or memories of the series or what it was about.)
They continue with their life in college, a younger series, and a scary
series, and a TV series followed. But now the author has written another
book about high school life and it is called *The Ruling Class*. It alternates between two students—the unpopular Myrna and the equally unpopular but new to the school Twyla. They call a group of the girls the
RCs, or the Ruling Class, and everyone wants to be one of them and no
one wants to cross them. They do things like tell someone a party is for-
mal and the person shows up in fancy dress while everyone else is in
jeans, or they tell a girl that a guy wants to meet her at the mall, but
instead the RCs are all in a car laughing and drive off and the girl stands
there with no boy in site. They are evil. Myrna the wannabe believes
she is a part of the RCs, but the new girl Twyla wants nothing to do with
them except to get revenge.

Alternate talk:

Let's say you are invited to this party and you were told to wear a de-
signer dress, but when you get there everyone is in jeans. This is just
one of the cruel tricks the RCs, or Ruling Class, of Highland Park High
School play on the girls they don't like because they don't wear the right
brand of clothes or even the right season of clothes.

Paulsen, Gary. 2003. *The Glass Café or, the Stripper and the State; How
My Mother Started a War with the System That Made Us Kind of Rich
and a Little Bit Famous*. New York: Wendy Lamb Books.
Grades 6–9

What kind of jobs do some of your parents have? (Wait for responses.)
Well, in *The Glass Café*, Tony's mom is a stripper. She is a single mom

with a college degree but finds she can make more money dancing than working with her English degree. One day Tony's art teacher talks about drawing the human body in class, and Tony gets the idea to go to his mom's work to draw the women there preparing for work. His art is soon on display and the government is soon at his door saying his mother is unfit. Since the rest of the title is *or, the Stripper and the State; How My Mother Started a War with the System That Made Us Kind of Rich and a Little Bit Famous* you know that there has to be a happy ending. This book is only 99 pages long. You can probably read it in about an hour.

---

Pavanel, Jane. 2001. *The Sex Book*. Montreal, Quebec: Lobster Press. Grades 9–12

(Use only if you are brave and you have an open-minded school.) The cover of this book reads, "The S Book" but part of a word is missing. I am not going to tell you what the title is, nor am I going to tell you what this book is about. You will have to figure that out for yourself, but it should be easy to figure out what words I can't say that start with the letter S. And please don't make any guesses out loud.

---

Peck, Richard. 2004. *The Teacher's Funeral: A Comedy in Three Parts*. New York: Dial Books. Grades 4–9

Do you think that someone who is 17, still has a year of high school left, and doesn't have a teaching certificate should be allowed to teach? (Hope they will say no. If they say "Yes," say, "Well so did this Indiana town.") Well, neither does Russell in *The Teacher's Funeral* by Richard Peck. In fact, he is hoping they won't hire a new teacher at all. Their teacher has died, and to save money the town decided to hire someone in high school rather than someone from the teacher's college. She will be getting paid a whole $36 a month. Keep in mind this is in 1904. There are a couple other conditions. One is that there has to be eight students at the school and there are only seven, so they have to recruit some others, even if they are maybe a little too old for school. Another is that she and her students have to pass a test, and she hopes they can show what they have learned and not mess things up for her and themselves.

---

Peters, Julie Anne. 2004. *Luna*. New York: Little, Brown.
Grades 8–12

A girl named Regan is having a slumber party. She is really afraid her brother is going to sneak down and ruin things. She is not afraid in the usual way, that he will try to scare them or steal their food or stomp on their things. She is afraid he will want to join them. He comes down and one of her friends offers to put nail polish on his fingers and toes. Most boys would be disgusted, but Regan's brother jumps at the chance. He even runs off to his room to bring back his own heart and butterfly stickers to put on the nails. Then when they start dancing, he starts dancing like no one has seen a guy dance before. Regan is humiliated. This is in front of her friends. Normally she will come home and find her brother in their private basement wearing makeup and dresses and a wig, but no one else can see but her. This time her friends might know that he is really a girl. He is a she and wants to be called Luna. Although he looks like a boy in all ways, he feels like a girl inside and wants to go shopping as a girl and to school as a girl and eventually become a girl, but he is not ready yet. His sister Regan is not ready for him to come out yet either.

Plum-Ucci, Carol. 2000. *The Body of Christopher Creed*. San Diego: Harcourt.
Grades 6–12

You hear stories about missing people in the news all the time. Before a murderer or kidnapper is found, if one is found, they usually question the family, friends, and coworkers and start search parties in nearby areas. You might remember the case of Laci Petersen, when her body showed up in the water? Or the case of Lori Hacking, whose body is still not discovered. But there was also a case that didn't get as much attention. You might remember that it happened in Wisconsin. Audrey Seiler faked her own kidnapping to gain attention from her boyfriend because the relationship was ending. She was caught on tape buying the supplies for her kidnapping. (Update with current stories from the news.) In the book *The Body of Christopher Creed*, clues aren't as obvious. A kind of nerdy boy, whom everyone makes fun of at school, just disappears. No one knows if he was killed or kidnapped or if he ran away. His neighbor has to find out and sets out to look for clues and piece it together himself, even by breaking into the guy's home to find his diary.

Plum-Ucci, Carol. 2003. *The She*. New York: Harcourt.
Grades 8–12

Now, for the sake of this story, let's say you know how to drive a boat even though there is no water around here. The man who runs the docks asks you if you will take these Girl Scouts out to show them how to drive a boat so they can earn their badges. You don't really want to, but you can't say no. You want to even less when you see that these Girl Scouts are your age. They are in high school. So you think it would be funny if you scare them and tip the boat. Only one girl doesn't come back up. She can swim, but no one can see her. She disappears. And the girl driving the boat swears she heard a loud shrieking noise when the girl went into the water. Evan heard this noise many years earlier when his parents contacted him by radio from their boat to tell him and his brother that there was trouble. His parents drowned as well. Many people from this town seem to drown and when it happens someone always hears the loud shrieking noise that is attributed to the sea monster everyone calls "The She." The Girl Scout incident was so devastating for Grey that she checked herself into a mental hospital, but she now seeks the help of Evan to find out of it really was a monster in the water that was taking all these people's lives. Or are people faking their own deaths to avoid drug trafficking charges, as others believe?

Alternate talk:

If I told you that I once saw a huge sea creature that devours boats, would you believe me? Well, you are not alone. *The She* by Carol Plum-Ucci starts with two boys who witness their parents' death at sea by radio. Some people swear that every time a boat goes down in these waters that there is a really loud shrieking noise, which is attributed to the sea. Evan hears such a noise the night his father dies.

Alternate talk:

Did you hear that? (Pretend to hear the shrieking of "The She.") Well, not many others have either.

Plum-Ucci, Carol. 2002. *What Happened to Lani Garver*. New York: Harcourt.
Grades 8–12

You may have seen the old *Saturday Night Live* skit about Pat. The joke is that no one can tell if Pat is a man or a woman, so they keep trying to ask him or her questions that might give them a hint as to whether he is a guy or a girl. Well, that's kind of what happens in the book *What Happened to Lani Garver*. A tall boy or girl is new to the school and two girls decide to find out. The new student is a drummer. Do you think that means a guy or a girl? Shoulder-length hair with the top layers bobbed under. Guy or girl? Six-foot tall? Guy or girl? Reads books. Guy or girl? Cleans his/her hands? Guy or girl? Dark eyelashes and peachy skin? Guy or girl? Finally Claire and her friend just come out and ask, and he says that he is not a girl, but he also doesn't say that he is a boy. Soon Claire becomes friends with him but their popular friends are not too happy about this, especially when they find out he is gay. Then one day there is trouble. There are disturbing phone calls and missing packages. And you have to decide what you think happened to Lani Garver.

---

Prue, Sally. 2002. *The Devil's Toenail*. New York: Scholastic.
Grades 6–10

You may have wished on a star or thrown a penny in a fountain or made a wish on an eyelash or maybe you have your own superstitions. The devil's toenail is a stone or fossil that is hollowed out and supposedly has some dark powers. After Stevie discovers this stone in *The Devil's Toenail*, he suddenly feels stronger. He feels like he can stand up to the boys at his new school who want him to steal and set fires. He thinks he can get away with anything, even hurting his sister.

---

Rackley, Virginia Ruth et al. 1997. *Ten Sisters: A True Story*. Mahomet, IL: Mayhaven.
Grades 9–12

How many of you are only children? How many have one brother or sister? Two? Three? Four? Five? Six? Seven? Eight? Nine? Ten? Eleven? No? Well try to think what it would be like to have 11 brothers and sisters living in your home? How about a two-room home? Not two bedrooms, but only two rooms. That is what the Waggoner sisters experienced, and each of them tells her own story in *Ten Sisters*. This is the story of a family of 14, ten sisters and two brothers. The brothers were older and were no longer living in the family. They ate rabbit for dinner and rarely had new clothes. All they got for Christmas was a half a piece of candy. When child services saw the way they were living, they assumed there could be no love and care and they separated all of them. Gradually they tried to find one another. (Continue with stories from the book that you found meaningful.)

---

Rees, Douglas. 2003. *Vampire High*. New York: Delacorte Press. Grades 6–10

Raise your hand if you would do your homework even if you were told you would still get an A if you didn't do it? What if you had to play a sport you didn't like to get the As? What if everyone at your school was a vampire—except you and the water polo team? Cody is not doing so well in school. His parents tell him that he has two choices. He can go to Our Lady of Perpetual Homework or Vlad Dracul Magnet School. Not wanting to do homework, he chooses Vlad Dracul. Soon he finds out that it is a school of vampires, and the only reason the school exists is because of the water polo team. The state says that all schools must have a water polo team, knowing that vampires can't go in the water and hoping this will close the school. They get away with this, however, by bringing failing humans in to join the water polo team and giving them As without their having to do any work.

---

Rennison, Louise. 2000. *Angus, Thongs, and Full-Frontal Snogging*. New York: HarperCollins. Grades 8–11

The title of this one, *Angus, Thongs, and Full-Frontal Snogging*, is a bit odd, but not if you know it is written by a British woman. In fact, the diary entries sound almost like those of Bridget Jones, if you have read those books or seen those movies. As for the title, Angus stands for her cat, you know what thongs are, and snogging is the word for kissing in England. Now Georgia is just like any other teenager, only her days seem a little more interesting. She accidentally shaves off her eyebrows. She protests wearing her beret at school. She has a crush on an older boy.

She gets mad when one of her friends rates her nose a zero out of 10 in a game they play. And she pays a boy to give her kissing lessons.

---

Rodman, Mary. 2004. *Yankee Girl*. New York: Farrar Straus Giroux. Grades 4–9

In 1964, in Mississippi, you would have found people who expected African Americans to move aside when you passed, drink from different glasses than you, expect to be called by their first names, and never have a white person introduce themselves, and not attend the same schools as white children. *Yankee Girl* is the story of a sixth-grade girl whose father is in the FBI. He has moved the family from Chicago to Mississippi to work during the civil rights movement. His daughter Alice finds the behavior of people in the South very strange. Her school is about to be one of the first in the area to be integrated, and a black girl named Valerie will soon be attending their school. She has to decide if she should treat this girl as she wants to and as her parents want her to, or if she should be cruel to her like the other girls in her class so she won't be left out. (Use with *Through My Eyes* by Ruby Bridges. )

Alternate talk:

You may have heard of people like Ruby Bridges who was one of the first black children to be integrated into white schools in the South . . .

---

Rosoff, Meg. 2004. *How I Live Now*. New York: Random House. Grades 7–12

Would you like it if your parents left you all alone for months? Most people would, and so did Daisy. Her mother died when giving birth to her, so she has never felt close to her father. Now her father has remarried and she doesn't want to be around when his new wife has their baby. So she takes off for England where she is going to stay with the aunt she never met—her mother's sister. There she meets her cousins, including a really good-looking one who drives and smokes even though he is only 14. Not long after she arrives, her aunt has to go on a quick trip to another country, which is just like going to another state in America. Only she doesn't return. While she is gone, war breaks out and Daisy and her cousins have to live by themselves. They are fine for a while. Daisy even starts falling in love with her cousin. But soon soldiers come to their door and their lives are changed forever.

Alternate talk:

Let's say you go to meet some relatives in another state or country and you are greeted by a 14-year-old boy who is smoking and says he is going to drive you to their home. Do you go? Well, maybe you shouldn't. This is what happens to Daisy.

---

Ryan, Pam Munoz. 2000. *Esperanza Rising*. New York: Scholastic. Grades 4–8

Think about the last person in the world you would ever want to marry. Now, what if you had a choice of being rich and married to this person or being poor and having to work and not go to school. Which would you choose? That is the choice Esperanza and her mother had to make in the book *Esperanza Rising*. Her father is a rancher in Mexico, and people who want his land kill him. They promise to let the family stay on the land as long as the mother marries one of the most influential men in the area, even though he is ugly and mean and disgusting. Her mother decides instead to sneak away to America with their servants to pick fruits and vegetables to survive. Now, Esperanza is used to telling her servants what to do and having them bathe her and dress her. And now she is a guest in their small home, which is something she can't get used to.

---

Satrapi, Marjane. 2003. *Persepolis: The Story of a Childhood*. New York: Pantheon. Grades 9–12

What stores do you buy your clothes at? I'm just curious. What stores are popular today for teenagers? Is it still the Limited and the Gap? (Name other stores if you get few responses. You may want to throw in some you know they don't shop at just to get responses, such as Laura Ashley.) Well, in some countries, as you know, they wouldn't have a choice. *Persepolis* is the story of a girl who is living in Iran during the Islamic Revolution. It is the author's true story, but it is told using pictures, like a comic book. One day she is going to school in 1980, and she is told she now has to start wearing a veil. Boys are separated from girls, and their class work becomes more religious. You think your dress code is bad. Think about what it would be like to come to school and be taught about religion and have to wear a uniform. This story is about a family fighting these new laws and the people around them who are killed for expressing their beliefs. Marjane Satrapi, the author, was stopped in the street and almost arrested for having music and modern clothing, and she had to lie to her friends and say that she prayed multiple times a day so no one would suspect that she was against the fundamentalist movement.

Alternate talk:

(Ask what music or items students would not be able to live without.)

---

Schupack, Deborah. 2003. *The Boy on the Bus*. New York: The Free Press.
Grades 9–12

What if one day you are coming home from school. You get off the bus or out of the car and walk inside your house and there is your mom, only she isn't your mom. Something is wrong with her. Instead of yelling at you to put your backpack in your room, she greets you with a plate of cookies. Instead of asking you if you passed the test, she asks you what you are planning to do this weekend. (You can invent your own scenarios.) This is not your mom. She looks like your mom, but something is not quite right. That is what Meg wonders about her son in the book *The Boy on the Bus*. One day her son refuses to get off the school bus. When he is off, she notices that something is different. His hair is different and his eyes aren't quite right. His asthma seems to have disappeared, and all of a sudden he is causing mischief, unlike her real son. She calls the boy's father and her daughter home to help her figure out what is wrong. Is the mother crazy? Is she imagining it? Or did something happen to that boy on the bus? (I hate to do this to teens, but the book did it to me: there is no obvious resolution, unless it was hidden from me and the reviewers, and, disappointingly, it appears that the boy is her son and she just is imagining the boy she once had or wanted to have.)

Sebold, Alice. 2002. *The Lovely Bones*. Boston: Little Brown.
Grades 9–12

If you could spy on anyone and find out anything you wanted to without his or her knowing, who would it be and what would you want to know? In *The Lovely Bones* by Alice Sebold, Susie has been raped and murdered at the age of 14. She dies, but her body is not ready to move on until she is done watching everyone she knows on Earth live without her, including her killer.

---

Sebold, Alice. 1999. *Lucky*. New York: Scribner.

Alice Sebold wrote the best-selling novel *Lovely Bones*. In *Lovely Bones* there is a rape. The author was raped when she was younger, and her book *Lucky* is the true story of this experience.

---

Shales, Tom, and James Andrew Miller. 2002. *Live from New York: An Uncensored History of Saturday Night Live*. Boston: Little, Brown.
Grades 9–12

How many of you have ever seen the show *Saturday Night Live*? Well, this book is about the history of the show from the point of view of most of the people who appeared on the show. It is almost 600 pages long, but the great thing about it is that you don't have to read it all. Just pick out the sections written by the people you like on the show. Maybe you'll want to read about Chris Rock or Adam Sandler. Just skim through and read the parts that interest you. One interesting fact was that Julia Sweeney created the androgynous character Pat based on someone she worked with. Her coworker told her she was still too feminine and that's when Pat came about. (Use other stories from the book that interest you or that would interest your students.)

Alternate talk:

(You could also start by mixing names from the book with those of other comedians and asking the kids if the people were on *Saturday Night Live* or not. For a more bleak option, you could also pull out names of performers from the show and ask if they are now alive or dead. For that option pair with the book *The Hollywood Book of Death: The Bizarre, Often Sordid, Passings of More Than 125 American Movie and TV Idols*.)

---

Sherwood, Ben. 2000. *The Man Who Ate the 747*. New York: Delacorte. Grades 9–12.

How long do you think you could kiss someone? In *The Man Who Ate the 747*, a man is a keeper of records. He works for something kind of like the *Guinness Book of World Records*. This particular assignment means watching two people kiss to make sure they don't separate their lips. His next assignment is to go visit the man who is eating a 747 airplane by grinding it to bits. The man is eating the 747 to win the love of a woman. But now he has competition, because the record keeper is falling in love with the same woman. (Ask about other world records.)

---

Simmons, Michael. 2003. *Pool Boy*. Brookfield, CT: Roaring Brook. Grades 7–12

Martha Stewart went to prison for insider trading. This is white collar crime. (Use more current examples, if available.) This is also what Brett's dad is found guilty of in *Pool Boy*. Brett was one of the rich kids in town, but now he has to give up his big house and job-free life, move in with his aunt on the wrong side of the tracks, and become the pool boy for people he knew, and even for the house he once lived in.

---

Slade, Arthur. 2003. *Dust*. New York: Random House Grades 6–12

Let's say you really needed to get somewhere, like to school or the mall or to a friend's party, and you had no way to get there. A stranger walks by and offers to give you a ride. Would you take the ride? Smart idea. Not only could you be robbed or attacked, but if you were one of the children in *Dust* by Arthur Slade, you might find that you just disappear to a place where no one can find you. And you might find that other people in your class soon start to disappear.

Alternate talk:

(Hold up a mirror and have some students take turns looking into it.) Now close your eyes, then open them, look in the mirror, and tell me what you see. (Most answers will probably be themselves, others, or objects in the room.) Well, in the book *Dust*, by Arthur Slade, people pack into a theatre to be able to look into the Mirror of All Things, where they see their dreams. A young girl might see dolls. A farmer might see rain. But you might also see trouble. (You might also ask students what dream they think they would see in the mirror.)

---

Slade, Arthur. *Tribes*. 2002. New York: Wendy Lamb Books.
Grades 7–12

Let's see if you can guess what kinds of students or people would be in each of the following cliques or social groups. The jocks? The teacher clique? Born agains? The cool and detached clique? The digeratis? Busybodies? Logos? The lipstick/hairspray clique? (Pause after each to wait for and offer answers.) These are some of the names that the guy in the book *Tribes* by Arthur Slade gives to the kids at his school. After losing his anthropologist father he withdraws from everyone at school and, instead, observes the different cliques in his school, giving them tribal names.

---

Smith, Cynthia Leitich. 2002. *Indian Shoes*. New York: HarperCollins.
Grades 3–6

Who wants to trade shoes with me? (Hopefully no one really will, or they will not when they realize you mean forever.) In the book *Indian Shoes*, a boy sees a pair of moccasins in an antique store with a sign that reads "$50 or best offer." When he realizes his grandfather misses his Native American home, he empties his savings and goes back to the store with just under $30, but a librarian has beat him there with $30 to offer. He decides to trade his high-top sneakers, instead. His sneakers now are displayed in the library with a sign that reads, "Traded from Ray Halfmoon, Cherokee Seminole High Tops, Not Indian Made, but Indian Worn (Guaranteed)." The rest of the stories all deal with Ray and his family. (This book would also be good for short read alouds).

---

Smith, Cynthia Leitich. 2001. *Rain Is Not My Indian Name*. New York: HarperCollins.
Grades 5–9

(Approach a student.) What is your nationality? (Wait for a reply.) Would you attend a summer camp with students who are all Polish? (It doesn't matter if they answer yes or no.) In the book *Rain Is Not My Indian*

*Name*, Rain's mother has died. Then her best friend dies. She doesn't really want to do anything, but a woman in the town has set up a summer camp for all the Native American teenagers in town, which happens to be only four. A woman running for office in town writes an editorial about how they should not be funding a camp for only a few students. After this editorial, Rain soon begins to participate.

---

Sones, Sonya. 2001. *What My Mother Doesn't Know*. New York: Simon Pulse.
Grades 7–12

Here is a question for the girls in the room. Let's say all your friends were on vacation for winter break. So no one knows that you have been hanging out with this kind of nerdy unattractive guy whom everyone calls Murphy, which is his last name. They even say things like "You're such a Murphy" to mean "You're such a jerk." But you got to know him in art class and then you ran into him over winter break. Then you got to spend a lot of time with him over the break, picking out a tree with his parents, going to a movie, and ice skating. You really like him. He's just not real cute. Everyone makes fun of him at school. What would you do when your friends got back in town. Would you tell them? Or would you end the relationship. (Wait for responses.) This is exactly what happens in the book *What My Mother Doesn't Know*. Sophie goes through several boyfriends. One was a creep she met online. One is really cute. But for some reason, she is more attracted to the weird, ugly guy at school whom no one likes. So now she has to decide if she should tell her friends the truth about the guy she met over break or if she should continue to ignore him in the hallways. This book is written in poetry form, only it doesn't sound like poems and you can probably read it in about an hour.

---

Soto, Gary. 2003. *The Afterlife*. Orlando: Harcourt.
Grades 6–10

Be careful when you compliment someone, especially if you are being sarcastic. In *The Afterlife*, Chuy tells a guy in the bathroom that he likes his yellow shoes. Chuy is now dead. But he isn't quite gone yet. He can look down on everyone from above and see his killer and how his family and friends are dealing with his death.

---

Soto, Gary. 1997. *Buried Onions*. San Diego: Harcourt.
Grades 7–12

"What are some of the things your parents ask you to do for them? (Common answers include cleaning your room, mowing the lawn, watching your brothers and sisters.) Well, I bet they never asked you to avenge the death of someone in the community by murdering the victim's killer? In *Buried Onions* by Gary Soto, Eddie's aunt wants him to do just that. But Eddie has different plans for his life, even though everything and everyone seem to get in his way." (Bromann, 1999:63)

---

Spinelli, Jerry. 2002. *Loser.* New York: Joanna Cotler Books.
Grades 4–7

Raise your hand if you think you can do the following things better than anyone in your class. Who can hit a telephone pole with a stone? Who can eat the most cupcakes? Who can go to bed the latest? You probably won't want to admit this, but who can weigh the most? Who can burp the loudest? (Let's hear you.) Who can grow the tallest? (Taken from page 6 of *Loser.* Invent more of your own.) These are the competitions that Zinkoff and his friends compete in every year only; Zinkoff never notices he doesn't win. He never notices people think of him as a loser because he is just happy to be a part of the games.

---

Spinelli, Jerry. 2000. *Stargirl*. New York: Alfred A. Knopf.
Grades 7–12

There's a strange new girl at school. She wears clothes that look like costumes from the past with long skirts. She plays her ukulele in the lunchroom and sings to people on their birthdays, and they have no idea how she knows it is their birthdays. And worse of all, she cheers for the wrong team in sports. She is just so happy when anyone scores that she cheers along. People wonder where she came from. But what is even stranger than the girl herself is that she is suddenly starting to get popular.

---

Springer, Nancy. 2003. *Blood Trail*. New York: Holiday House.
Grades 6–10

One day Jeremy and his friend Aaron were out together, and Aaron looked a little different. Aaron revealed to Jeremy that he was afraid of his own brother. Jeremy didn't say any more, but all day he tried to call Aaron—until he heard an ambulance down the street. His friend Aaron had been stabbed over 70 times, and Jeremy has to decide if he should tell the police what his friend had told him in the book *Blood Trail*.

Alternate talk:

Have you ever kept a secret before? In the book *Blood Trail*, Jeremy has to decide if he should tell the police what he knows about his friend's death.

---

Tarbox, Katie. 2000. *Katie.com: My Story*. New York: Dutton.
Grades 7–12

Let's say you are on a class trip rooming with one of your best friends, and she tells you that she has arranged to meet this guy she met on the Internet in a particular hotel room right now. Would you let her go? (Wait for responses.) What would you do? Well, Katie's friend does the same thing in *Katie.com* by Katherine Tarbox. All her friends seem to have abandoned her for boyfriends and popularity, and she has no one to talk to anymore except this guy she met on the Internet who seems to understand her so well. He tells her he is 23, then 31, and then she finds out he is 41. She goes to that hotel room, although she tells her friend the room number. Luckily her mom and others come to get her before something even worse happens. Now she has to deal with the reactions of her classmates in school. This is the true story of what happened to Katie Tarbox. You may have seen her on TV shows like *Oprah* or read about her in magazines. She also has a Web site katiet.com.

Alternate talk:

(Start with recent stories in the news about teenagers getting into trouble after meeting someone on the Internet.)

Tashjian, Janet. 2003. *The Gospel According to Larry*. New York: Laurel Leaf.
Grades 7–12

Let's say you had to get rid of most everything you own and only keep 75 items. Socks count for two items. So this means your clothes and backpack and CDs and everything you own counts. What are some of the things you would keep? (Wait for responses.) In *The Gospel According to Larry*, Larry kind of preaches on his beliefs about the world and keeps them on his Web site, www.thegospelaccordingtolarry.com, which, by the way, is a real Web site. But no one knows who he really is, not even his friends, who worship him and who might not be so thrilled to find out he is keeping this secret. On his Web site he gives hints of who he is by revealing his 75 items, and when he acquires a new item, he has to take one away.

---

Testa, Maria. 2003. *Almost Forever*. Cambridge, MA: Candlewick.
Grades 4–10

(Use the beginning I created for short books from *Booktalking That Works*.) Let's say your friend comes up to you before school and asks you what book you read for your book report. You say, "What book report?" He says, "The one that's due today. Seventh hour." You completely forgot and run to the library to find the shortest book you can find, and you find *Almost Forever* by Maria Testa. I read this book in about 20 minutes before a class and during the break. It is written in poetry form, but it reads like a novel. In the story, a family gets a letter that their father has to go be a doctor in the Vietnam War. Now letters from their father come every day, until one day they stop.

---

Thomas, Rob. 1996. *Rats Saw God*. New York: Simon & Schuster.
Grades 8–12

How many of you belong to a club or sport at this school? In the book *Rats Saw God*, Steve decides to start a club that wouldn't make his father very happy. He calls it GOD for Grace Order of Dadaists. They wear t-shirts that read "Go with God" and have a pamphlet that reads "God Isn't for Everyone." Steve wasn't always like this; he is now failing his classes even though he has one of the highest test scores in the school. He went from honor student to stoner. And now, in order to pass his English class, he has to write a 100-page essay about his father, his old girlfriend, and life at his old school until the present. So after you read his journal, you will find out why Steve hates his father and what made Steve leave Texas in such a hurry.

Alternate talk:

DID YOUR SECOND GRADE TEACHER SCOLD YOU FOR COL-ORING AN APPLE PURPLE AND THE SKY RED, THUS DESTROY-ING YOUR ARTISTIC URGES? . . . DO PREDICTABLE, MUNDANE, ORDINARY, COMMON AND ROUTINE SOUND LIKE BAD WORDS TO YOU? If SO, GO WITH GOD (p. 30).

God is the club . . . (Include part of summary above.)

Alternate talk:

Steve has been failing his classes although he used to get As. He fled Texas because of what he saw in a window one night. He couldn't find his girlfriend. He begged her friend to tell him where she was. He still couldn't find her. He was so upset. Then he went to see his teacher . . .

Thomas, Rob. 1997. *Slave Day*. New York: Simon & Schuster. Grades 7–12

Can you think of someone in school you would love to be able to order around and have as your slave for just one day? Don't mention any names. Well, if you went to Robert E. Lee High in the book *Slave Day* by Rob Thomas you would be able to participate in the annual Slave Day event, and if you had enough money you could buy one of your teachers or classmates and make that person your slave for the day. Some of those on auction are "an activist, a football player, a hated teacher, a sensitive guy, a cheerleader, the most popular girl in school, and a com-puter nerd. One will fall in love. One will find out he's not as washed up as he thought he was. One will find out that he's a little smarter than he thought he was. And one will get a little lucky" (Adapted from Bromann, 1999:62).

Thompson, Craig. 2004. *Blankets.* Marietta, GA: Top Shelf.
Grades 11–12

Now this book may appear to be pretty long. It is almost 600 pages. A book like this would probably take you days to read. However, this is a graphic novel, and there are more pictures than words. It only took me about two hours to read. I can't really tell you what it is about since it is about nothing. At least, that's what the author says on his Web site. He said he wanted it to be more about an emotional experience than a plot. It is basically the story of a boy from his childhood to adulthood and how he struggled with fitting in at school and even at church camp. There he meets a girl from another state who becomes his first love. He goes to visit her and thinks he has found his future, but he is wrong. The story alternates between his present and his childhood, tying together different situations in his life. (Background information from www.dootdoot garden.com/dootdoot.htm)

Thompson, Julian F. 1983. *The Grounding of Group 6.* New York: Henry Holt.
Grades 7–12

You know how on talk shows they send teens to boot camp to change their ways. Well, in the *Grounding of Group 6* by Julian Thompson, this group of teens is sent away to what they think will be like a boot camp to help them reform. What they don't know is that the camp leaders have been hired by their parents to make sure that they never return.

Alternate talk:

(Start by asking the students what punishments they have received from their parents either in their teenage years or as children.)

Trueman, Terry. 2004. *Cruise Control.* New York: HarperCollins.
Grades 5–10

If you have read the book *Stuck in Neutral*, this is another side of the story. *Stuck in Neutral* was told from the point of view of a boy with cerebral palsy who could not talk, and no one knew how smart he was because all he could do was make noises. *Cruise Control* is written from the point of view of his brother, who can talk. His brother thinks he got all the talent from his disabled brother and has no idea that he can hear and understand him. In the first book, the boy thinks his father wants to kill him. In this book, the brother reveals what he really wants to have happen to his brother.

---

Trueman, Terry. 2003. *Inside Out*. New York: HarperCollins. Grades 7–11

Zach's doctor asks him a question. He asks him if he would be more upset to find out his mother died or that the candy machine is out of candy bars. Zach asks the doctor, "Would they put more candy bars in the machine pretty soon?" (p. 39). Zach loves his mother, he thinks, and his mother is good to him, but Zach has schizophrenia. He has voices in his head that call him names. He can't tell right from wrong or good from bad, and he can't detect sarcasm or fear. So he is not afraid when he is taken hostage in a store by two teenagers with guns.

---

Trueman, Terry. 2000. *Stuck in Neutral*. New York: HarperCollins. Grades 5–10

This is the story of a boy named Shawn. He is 15, but he can't move and he can't talk. He has cerebral palsy. What people don't know is that he can hear and read and understand. And because of this, he knows that his father is planning to kill him. (You could continue with how he knows his father plans to kill him by what the dad says about ending his pain and about his appearance on a talk show, but this brief talk and the brevity of the book make it appealing as it is.)

---

Truss, Lynne. 2003. *Eats, Shoots & Leaves*. New York: Gotham Books Grades 10–12

Here's a joke for you. (This is not taken directly from the text.) A panda walks into a bar (change bar to restaurant if not appropriate for your school) and he eats, (pause) shoots a gun, (pause) and leaves. Everyone in the bar looks at each other and the panda comes back in. One man asks, "What did you do that for?" The panda says, "Well, I was looking in the encyclopedia and it says that a panda eats, shoots, and leaves." Obviously the panda mixed up its punctuation and added a comma. The entry should have read that a panda eats shoots and leaves. Punctuation may not be that exciting to you. The author of this book agrees that it is not that exciting to many people, and that is why so many signs you see are written inaccurately. The sentence "A woman, (say the word comma) without her man, is nothing" is much different from the phrase "A woman: (say the word colon) without her, man is nothing." The first indicates that a woman needs a man and the second that a man needs a woman. They both have the same words but the punctuation changes the meaning. There is even a group called the Apostrophe Protection Society that writes letters to businesses or people who have misspelled signs. So if you want your teacher to stop putting all those red marks on your paper when you add too many commas or when you are missing too many apostrophes, you might want to read this book. It is a fun way to look at punctuation.

---

Tyche. 2004. *Vampire Dreams*. New York: Spark.
Grades 9–12

(You might start by asking students to define words from the book or by asking if they plan to take the SATs and how they will prepare.) If you need to prepare for the SATs you might try reading a book like *Vampire Dreams*, which uses words that frequently appear on the SAT tests to tell the story about a vampire who may be on the loose again. The definitions for the words are even at the bottom of each page.

---

Van Belkom, Edo, ed. 2000. *Be Afraid: Tales of Horror*. Toronto, Ontario: Tundra Books.
Grades 4–10

Have you ever seen an old episode of *The Twilight Zone*? There was one I always remember about the woman who wants to have plastic surgery because she thinks she is ugly, but in the end they show her before her surgery as a beautiful woman and all the doctors and nurses are pigs. (Use examples from your own favorite episodes.) Then there was one I don't remember but that was mentioned in this book *Be Afraid! Tales of Horror*, where a woman thinks she has aliens in her attic, but they are really astronauts. I would still have to sleep with the lights on if I watched one of those shows today. That is the basis for one of the stories in this book. This boy loves *The Twilight Zone*. He wants to watch a marathon on TV but his parents think he should be trick or treating. So he reluctantly agrees and follows these kids he meets until he comes to a house where the man is watching *The Twilight Zone*. The man offers to let the boy watch with him, and the boy goes into the house, which is even more dangerous than the shows he has seen on TV. This is just one of the many kinds of scary stories that could really happen.

---

Vande Velde, Vivian. 1997. *Curses, Inc. and Other Stories*. New York: Bantam Doubleday Dell.
Grades 4–9

You have probably been searching the Internet before and have come across a link to a site that you wanted to take a look at. So you click on the site out of curiosity. Maybe it is the "Are you smarter than J Lo?" quiz or "The Love Calculator" or "Magic 8 Ball." Or maybe it is "Curses, Inc." In the book *Curses, Inc. and Other Stories*, the title story is about a boy who has just been humiliated by the girl he won't take to the dance because he doesn't want to spend his money on her. He'd rather spend it on computer games. Well, one day he is surfing the Internet and he comes across a site called Curses, Inc. He thinks it will be one of those joke sites, or for a nominal fee he might get to send someone a certificate that says they have been cursed. So he plays around with it, making selections from all the categories. He can choose from a jinx, hex, geas, bane, or a malediction. (If you want a longer talk or to use this as a story, you might read the definition of each of these services. You could also ask students to choose the type of spell he should put on the girl.) He got to choose how long the spell would last and that it should involve bodily functions and warts. When he submitted his request the cost was $575. Still, believing this was a joke, he decided to choose a less-expensive curse. He opts for the temporary loss of her pet dog. When he gets to school he finds out it was very temporary. The dog was only gone a few seconds. He goes back to the computer to find a curse that would be even worse. Only he becomes a little addicted to the curses, making more than a couple requests, until he finds himself cursed. (This also works well as a read aloud or as storytelling by reading and paraphrasing.)

---

Vande Velde, Vivian. 1995. *The Rumpelstiltskin Problem*. New York: Scholastic.
Grades 4–10

You remember the telephone game from when you were a kid? (You could play it with them if you are brave, but some clever child might intentionally change the message to something sexual or crude. This is from Vande Velde's introduction.) You whisper something in someone's ear and everyone passes it on from ear to ear. It changes throughout the process, and the last person usually says something different from the first person. That is how fairy tales developed. The stories were passed on from person to person and not written down until years later. Because of this, they often don't make any sense. For example, Rumpelstiltskin. If the miller's daughter could turn straw into gold, then wouldn't the king ask them why they were poor if they could do such a thing? Why would she want to marry the king if he wants to chop her head off if she doesn't spin straw into gold? He'd want to chop her head off any time she didn't do things to his satisfaction. Then comes Rumpelstiltskin. He takes her ring in exchange for his turning the room of straw into gold? Now why would a man who can turn straw into gold need a ring? Now the girl has run out of things to give, so being the great parent she will be someday, she offers up her firstborn in exchange for more gold.

---

Vizzini, Ned. 2004. *Be More Chill*. New York: Hyperion.
Grades 9–12

If you wanted to give someone advice on how to be more cool, what do you think they could do? (Wait for responses.) Well, in *Be More Chill*, the answer is in a pill. Jeremy has friends, he is in the school play, and girls do talk to him, as friends, but he wants more. His father even asks him if he is gay. So one day Jeremy is at a party and this cool guy comes up and talks to him and tells him he has a solution to his problem. He has a pill called a squib that has a computer inside that will help him be cooler. The only problem is that it will cost him $600. Jeremy is not so sure he should pay for something that might just be aspirin, and he doesn't have the money. So he gets online to do two things. The first is to look up a squib. He finds it. It is real. Sony is manufacturing pills with computers inside, but he still can't find out if $600 is too much to pay. So he goes on eBay to look up squib and see if $600 is a fair price, only he comes across a Beanie Baby® called a squib instead. This sparks an idea. His aunt has beanie babies in her attic. He will offer to clean her gutters so he can steal the babies, sell them on eBay, and get his pill. Some of those beanie babies are going for thousands of dollars. So he does it. He makes his money. Now he needs to get the pill, and the pill actually works. A voice that sounds like Keanu Reeves starts to talk to him and give him advice on how to be more chill. The author of this book, Ned Vizzini, has been publishing essays in newspapers since he was in high school and put the memories of his high school life together in a book called *Teen Angst? Naaah . . . A Quasi-autobiography* (Vizzini, 2000). *Be More Chill* was on *Entertainment Weekly's* list of the top ten best books of 2004.

---

Waggoner, Susan. 2004. *It's a Wonderful Christmas: The Best of the Holidays 1940–1965*. New York: Stewart, Tabori Chang.
Grades 9–12

Raise your hand if you got a Hula-Hoop for Christmas this year? An Etch-a-Sketch? A Mr. Potato Head? The Game of Life? A Frisbee? Play-Doh? No one? Really? What did you get? Well, I am not that old really, but from 1940–1965 children were actually excited to get these toys for Christmas. (Use one of your own Christmas or holiday stories.) I remember wanting a Cabbage Patch Doll, but I got a fake one my mom's friend made instead. In the book *It's a Wonderful Christmas*, you will not only find out what gifts were popular during these years, but how people celebrated the holidays and other songs and items that were popular during this time.

---

Wallace, Rich. 2003. *Restless: A Ghost's Story*. New York: Viking.
Grades 8–12

How many of you would be brave enough to go to a cemetery by yourself at night? What if you brought a friend? What if you saw a strange light that seemed to be following you as you ran? What if you actually saw a ghost? (Have students raise their hands in response.) In *Restless*, by Rich Wallace, a boy does go jogging through the cemetery. He didn't like his soccer coach so he joined both cross country and football instead, so he uses the cemetery as a place to practice. He also likes to feel the presence of his brother who died when he was his age many years ago. But now when he goes there, there really is a light following him and one day he actually sees a ghost.

---

Watt, Alan. 2000. *Diamond Dogs.* New York: Warner Books.
Grades 10–12

Do you think your parents would lie for you? Well, in *Diamond Dogs*, Neil leaves a party drunk in his father's car. He decides to play that game where he sees how far he can drive with his lights off. Then he hears a thud. He stops. He gets out. He has killed the boy he just gave a wedgie to and thrown a bottle at while at the party. He puts the boy in the trunk of his car and goes home. The next day he goes to get the body and it is gone. He knows his father, the sheriff in charge of the case, is the one who took it.

Alternate talk:

(You could also start by asking the students to put themselves in the situation of the party and then ask what they would do if they accidentally hit someone with their car.)

---

Werlin, Nancy. 2004. *Double Helix.* New York: Dial Books.
Grades 8–12

There has been a lot in the news lately about stem-cell research. It has become very political because many people don't want it to happen, and many other people think it could help save lives. In *Double Helix*, a boy comes across a letter in his father's drawer that says something about a test for Huntington's disease as being negative. This makes Eli wonder what is going on. His mom is in a nursing home with this disease. So he goes to confront the doctor whose name is on this letter. Instead of answers, he gets a job. But this job gets him to secret places like an elevator that goes to a basement level no other elevator goes to and a girl who looks just like his mother.

---

Weyn, Suzanne. 2004. *Bar Code Tattoo.* New York: Scholastic.
Grades 6–12

You might have to show IDs at your school to get into the library or get into football games. But some schools are even starting to scan students' fingerprints as identification. (Tell stories of places you may have had your fingerprint scanned, such as the tanning salon or a bank.) Something similar happens to Kayla at her school. When they turn 17, they are now eligible to get a bar code tattoo. This tattoo is like a driver's license, credit card, ATM card, insurance card, and everything all in one. You no longer need to carry a wallet full of cards, and no one can steal them because the bar code tattoo is your identification. Only Kayla doesn't want one, and although it seemed optional, she soon finds out that not getting one causes trouble and danger for her and her family. There might be more to this tattoo than just identification.

---

Whelan, Gloria. 2000. *Homeless Bird*. New York: HarperCollins. Grades 4–9

In 1998, there was an article in the *New York Times* newspaper about a town called Vrindavan, India, where women are supposedly discarded by their families when they are widowed. Gloria Whelan, the author of *Homeless Bird*, read this article and decided to write a book about it. In her story, Koly has had a marriage arranged for her but her young husband soon dies. Her new mother-in-law puts her to work until her father-in-law dies. Then she is taken to this town where she is left on her own to survive. Although there was an article about this in the *New York Times*, I have heard women from India say that this is not true anymore. They say that women no longer are taken and left in Vrindavan.

---

Wicker, Christine. *Lily Dale: The True Story of the Town That Talks to the Dead*. 2003. New York: HarperCollins. Grades 8–12

I need at least three people to write a question on a piece of paper. It should be something you want to know about, something I wouldn't know, or something you want to know about your future. I won't even look at the questions. I will just hold the papers to my forehead and give you an answer. (Ask an audience member ahead of time if he or she will help you. Tell the person you will be playing a psychic game and need help. Ask that person to tell you ahead of time what question he or she will be writing down and to put an X on it after it is folded. You could also find out the answer if there is one, but it doesn't matter since the trick is knowing the question. During the presentation ask at least three people to write down questions. The questions could be something they want to stump the booktalker with or something about the future they want to know. You have only seen the question of the one helper from the audience. Ask them to fold the questions. Do not look at them. Put them on a table, in your assistant's hand, or in a bag, box, or hat. Pull out one of the questions that does not have an X, that is NOT the one you took from the person assisting you. Do not look at it, but place it on your forehead. You don't even have to open it if it is not a sticky note. You could just hold it and stare at the closed paper. Do not look at this question. Pretend it is the question you already know about and say it out loud. The audience member pretends to be amazed. Now open the paper and read the question silently, pretending you were right. Or read it out loud, only replace it with the question you knew about ahead of time. You now have a glimpse at the next question. Throw that paper out and take a new one, but answer the last question you saw. You will have to make up an answer but the audience member will be amazed you could figure out his or her question since he or she didn't tell you. Only one person is helping you. This could be a teacher in a classroom. So, basically you are always answering the question on the previous piece of paper, except the audience does not know that when you started you did not answer the question that was actually written on the first piece of paper. The last question you choose should be the question from your audience helper, which you have already answered, but you will still be pretending it is the last question you looked at while answering the previous question. Answer the questions. Wait for groans or laughs.) Of course I am not very good at this, but I might be if I lived or summered in a town called Lily Dale, New York. Since the early-twentieth century, psychics and mediums and people who want to know their future have come to Lily Dale; now they come every summer. Christine Wicker, a former reporter for *Dallas Morning News* writes about this in the book called *Lily Dale*. What I just did with you was called billets. Now some people do this successfully, but others are fakes. Some would put a plant in the audience and answer the first fake question. After that, the reader already knows what the next question will be. Some claim to make tables dance, but the author discovers that a table was just top heavy. Others have had people hidden in rooms or used a tiny pencil on their wrists to write messages from the dead. But some seem to know things others don't. In fact, the author of this book was told by one medium about a family member she didn't even know existed until she researched it and found it to be true. She was told that no one could be right all the time. Is it real or fake? Are some real or fake? *Lily Dale* will help you decide. (Feel free to insert other interesting occurrences you picked up from this book. Mention famous people who went to Lily Dale. Mention the popular psychic John Edwards, who spoke there.)

Wild, Margaret. 2001. *Jinx*. New York: Walker.
Grades 8–12.

You probably have had boy trouble before. Maybe you dated someone and then caught him with your best friend. Maybe you find out he still collects Pokémon cards. Or you find out he has been exchanging his pictures with other girls on the Internet. But Jen in *Jinx*, by Margaret Wild, has a different problem. Her boyfriends keep dying on her. And so she gets the name Jinx.

Alternative talks:

(Ask what dating trouble students have had in the past. Mention all the dating shows on TV and how bad the dates are and then say how they are not as bad as Jen's dates.)

---

Wild, Margaret. 2004. *One Night*. New York: Alfred A. Knopf.
Grades 8–12

One night Gabe's stepmother goes to parent conferences at his school and goes into the bathroom only to find tons of writing on the wall with comments about her stepson, such as "I've been dumped by Gabe Fellows," and "Gabe Fellows screws around." One night a baby shows up at Gabe's door. He reads the note that says the baby is his. He has no idea who the mother is. *One Night* is a story in poems about a girl and a boy who have to make decisions about their lives after the girl finds out she is pregnant.

---

Winick, Judd. 2000. *Pedro and Me*. New York: Henry Holt.
Grades 9–12

How many of you watch, or have seen, the show *The Real World* on MTV? Which seasons did you see? Did any of you see or hear about the season in San Francisco? (Use your own memories.) This was the first season I was allowed to watch, so I especially remember the weird guy Puck who was a bicycle messenger and always causing problems and yelling and eating peanut butter from the jar and picking his nose. But the season was really more about Pedro. Pedro was gay and he had AIDS. MTV warned the other housemates that they would be living with someone with AIDS. Judd became his roommate. In fact, he became one of his closest friends. Judd is a cartoonist, so he put together this graphic novel called *Pedro and Me* about his experiences with Pedro on and after the show. Pedro was an AIDS activist and talked about how to prevent and live with the disease. When Pedro was too sick to go to speaking engagements, Judd took over. Pedro fell in love during the show and had a commitment ceremony with a man named Sean. Because of the illustrations, this book is like watching an episode of the *Real World* only it shows what went on behind the scenes.

Wittlinger, Ellen. 2004. *Heart on My Sleeve*. New York: Simon & Schuster.
Grades 9–12

How many of you use e-mail or instant messaging? Do you ever e-mail people who don't live in your town or state? In *Heart on My Sleeve*, Chloe goes to visit a college and meets a guy she really likes, only she won't be able to spend much time with him until she starts to go to school there next year, so they start an e-mail, letter, and instant-message relationship. This book is their correspondence with each other and their other friends and their families written entirely in those forms of communication. The long-distance relationship isn't the only problem. Chloe already has a boyfriend.

Alternate talk:

Do long-distance relationships work?

Wittlinger, Ellen. 2002. *The Long Night of Leo and Bree*. New York: Simon Pulse.
Grades 7–12

You hear stories in the news almost every week about missing children. Some are kidnapped and some are murdered. (Insert a brief story about a recent murder or kidnapping.) In *The Long Night of Leo and Bree*, Leo's sister was killed by her boyfriend. He can't get over it. One day he sees a girl walking down the street by a bar and thinks she probably deserved to die more than his good sister, so he decides to kidnap her.

Wolff, Virginia Euwer. 1993. *Make Lemonade*. New York: Henry Holt.
Grades 7–12

How many of you have ever babysat before? Keep your hands raised if
you would babysit even if it meant you couldn't study for a test and you
might fail. Keep your hands raised if you would babysit even if this were
the third time you would fail a test because you couldn't study because
you had to babysit. Keep your hands raised if you would babysit because
it is the child of your 17-year-old best friend, who has no one else. Keep
your hands raised if you would babysit even if your parents and counse-
lor told you not to. Keep your hands raised if you would babysit even if
you wouldn't get paid. Keep your hands raised if you would end up giving all your babysitting money back to the 17-year-old single mother you
babysit for. This is the problem LaVaughn faces in *Make Lemonade* by
Virginia Euwer Wolff. She has to decide if she should help a friend or
be the first person in her family ever to go to college.

---

Wyman, Carolyn. 2004. *Better Than Homemade*. Philadelphia: Quirk.
Grades 7-12

Name a food that is fast to make that you would buy in a store. *Better
Than Homemade* is a book about all those products that made life easier.
You will find out that the Twinkie was originally made with banana fill-
ing but it was changed to vanilla during a wartime banana shortage. And
that Shirk's Glazed Peanuts changed it's name to Beer Nuts when bar
owners realized they made people thirsty for more beer. Dou you remember Tang? It actually was not invented for the astronauts, but NASA
did contact the company to suggest that Tang could be a useful space
product. (Tell additional or alternate stories from the book.)

---

Youngs, Bettie B., and Jennifer Leigh Youngs. 2002. *Taste Berries for
Teens #3*. Deerfield Beach, FL: Health Communications, Inc.
Grades 7–12

Raise your hand if you agree with the following statements. "Don't date
your sister's ex-boyfriend." "There is love after your first love." "You can
be friends with your first love." "You can't have a boyfriend in seventh
grade." "Your parents will like your intelligent but heavily body-pierced
friend with multicolored hair if they just get to know him and his intel-
ligence." "Everyone should try out for the team." "You don't have to agree

with what your friends say." These are just some of the stories and advice from teenagers across the United States, who contributed their stories to *Taste Berries for Teens*.

Alternate talk:

(Ask students first for their advice to other teenagers. Expand on the stories or focus on just one.)

## REFERENCES

Bissinger, H. G. 2004. *Friday Night Lights*. Cambridge, MA: De Capo Press.

Bridges, Ruby. 1999. *Through My Eyes*. New York: Scholastic.

Bromann, Jennifer. 1999. "The Toughest Audience on Earth." *School Library Journal 45, no. 10* (October): 60–63.

Burns, John. 1998. "Once Widowed in India, Twice Scorned." *New York Times*. March 29, sec. 1, p. 1, col. 1.

Cabot, Meg. 2000. *The Princess Diaries*. New York: Harper Avon.

Danziger, Paula, and Ann M. Martin. 1998. *P.S. Longer Letter Later*. New York: Scholastic.

"Fiction Books of the Year." 2004. *Entertainment Weekly*. (December): 142.

Gupta, Vidya B. 1998. "Indian Widows." *New York Times*. March 30, p. A22.

Hinton, S. E. 1997. *The Outsiders*. New York: Puffin Books.

———. 1975. *Rumble Fish*. New York: Laurel Leaf.

———. 1979. *Tex*. New York: Dell.

Jenkins, Jerry, and Tim LaHaye. 2000. *Left Behind*. Wheaton, IL: Tyndale House.

Jimenez, Francisco. 2001. *Breaking Through*. Boston: Houghton Mifflin.

Levine, Gail Carson. 1997. *Ella Enchanted*. New York: Harper Trophy.

Lowry, Lois. 1993. *The Giver*. Boston: Houghton Mifflin.

Nelson, Peter. 1994. *Treehouses: The Art and Craft of Living Out on a Limb*. Boston: Houghton Mifflin.

Nilsen, Alleen Pace. 1979. "The House That Alice Built." *School Library Journal 26, no. 2:* 109–112.

Owen, David. 2002. *Hidden Secrets*. Buffalo, NY: Firefly.

Rodman, Mary. 2004. *Yankee Girl*. New York: Farrar Straus Giroux.

Susman, Gary. 2004. "It Takes a Village." *Entertainment Weekly* (August 10).

Traig, Jennifer. 2004. *Devil in the Details: Scenes from an Obsessive Girl-hood*. New York: Little, Brown.

Vizzini, Ned. 2000. *Teen Angst? Naaah: A Quasi-autobiography*. Minneapolis, MN: Free Spirit Press.

William, Kate. 1983. *Sweet Valley High: Double Love*. Lakeville, CT: Grey Castle Press.

# Booktalks Indexed by Genre/Theme

# Booktalks Indexed by Title

# About the Author

Jennifer Bromann is the library department chair at Lincoln-Way Central High School in New Lenox, Illinois. Her previous position was as head of youth services at Prairie Trails Public Library in Burbank, Illinois. Bromann is also an adjunct instructor at Joliet Junior College and at Northern Illinois University, where she is pursuing her doctorate in reading. This is her third book with Neal-Schuman. Contact Jennifer at bromannj@hotmail.com.

OT 71 X 334